The Confused Freelancer's Guide To Technology (1st Ed.)

THE BARE ESSENTIALS (AND MORE) *YOU* NEED TO GET YOUR FREELANCE BUSINESS ONLINE — AND BE YOUR OWN I.T. DEPARTMENT

Daniel S. Rosehill

The Freelancer's Guide To Technology (1st Ed.)
© Daniel Rosehill

By: Daniel S. Rosehill (BCL, MA)

ISBN-13: 9798651011919

V1.6

For permissions, to reproduce this work in part, please contact: legal@danielrosehill.com

FORWARD

A WORD ABOUT THE VALUE OF COLLABORATION

It seems a little strange to open a book about technology with a dedication. But to overcome my reticence to do so:

This book is dedicated to the many freelancers, spread across many countries (and several continents) who have been generous enough to share with me some of the wisdom that they have gleaned while pounding this unconventional path through life and employment.

I have received countless tiny nuggets of wisdom from many different sources over the years: Face-to-face meetings over coffee (sometimes beer), internet groups, Facebook groups, and email exchanges — to name but a few. Much of it has touched upon the sometimes delicate business of making this way of life 'work' — both the obvious details (you need a website!) as well as the subtleties (should you enforce a limit for client revisions? If so, what's a good number?). And the countless other fine details one needs to accumulate and grasp in order to make the whole self-employment picture work.

The tumultuous period during which I am writing this, in which the normal social fabric that underpins our societies has been so dramatically altered by a global public health crisis, has given me some pause for thought about where this freelancing business is all going. Both for me and the many others in similar situations. It is a crisis which has both shone a stark light upon the advantages of freelancing — remote technology is here, Zoom works (almost) flawlessly, and many of us don't *need* to be physically present at a worksite in order to get the job done! And which, at the same time, somewhat paradoxically, has underscored its deficiencies (many of those working from home for the first time have not been thrilled with the results!). And so, instead of worrying about the usual fine details of client management, prospecting methodologies, and exploring new sub-niches, I have been thinking about more global concerns for a change. And seeking answers to questions. How can we, as freelancers, best fit within the global economy (assuming we plan on maintaining updated skill-sets and committing to this path for the long term, that is)? Through working for a constantly fluctuating potpourri of clients? Or should they instead strive to maintain a core stable roster of them, possibly returning to one in-house after a period of time? Will HR departments, in the future, look more favorably upon those criss-crossing between the two worlds? Does doing so even carry a stigma now? And what about benefits — an issue which can make freelancing more trying when freelancers, as they occasionally do, find themselves unable to work due to a medical issue. Will the self-employed and freelancers ever be entitled to benefits — both from their governments and the companies they work for? There are others. I'll be the first to admit that I'm not sure what my own long-term evolution will look like — who can predict the future? — but questions like these, and others, are those which those beginning the freelance journey now might already be wondering.

While the answers to these questions might be unknowable, at least at the moment, they are nevertheless worth exploring — and especially at this juncture. Because if the forecasts and trend-predictors are correct and we really emerge into a world dominated by distributed teams, semi-remote offices, and a surge in the ranks of the world's freelancers, temporary employees, and the self-employed, then we will need to figure out a way to maintain some semblance of cohesiveness while working *with* one another but physically apart.

As freelancers, we will need to figure out a best way to grow within this paradigm — to thrive (rather than survive from month to month) and to achieve professional development in some process that should ideally mirror the kind of evolution we might expect were we working in-house growing through a succession of roles for one company.

And there might be other questions worth answering too — depending upon one's individual situation. Does being proximate to one's key target markets matter any more — so that a cup of coffee can be drunk with a lead without having to transverse the Atlantic Ocean to do so? Or are we moving into an era in which physical geography is wholly irrelevant: an online meritocracy of sorts in which office politics and location become subordinate, as perhaps they always should, to one's skillset and ability to deliver raw value to one's customer(s)? These dynamics will all be taking place against an interesting backdrop. The rising tide of AI can be expected to condense, perhaps greatly so, the pool of vocations which thinking humans are even called upon to undertake in the first place. And in that sense, AI will be an equal opportunities discriminator, affecting both freelancers and salaried employees equally.

These are more questions than these that remain unresolved — both for me and, I think many. But one certitude I have drawn from the experience is the power of connectivity and collaboration even when meetings, as right now, can't be facilitated face-to-face.

While it may strike some as obvious, I have been wowed by the amount of encouragement, information, and solidarity which can be shared and gleaned during a simple Zoom meeting with somebody across an ocean who is also in the business of freelancing. Sometimes, I will admit, these interactions have been mildly discouraging. For instance I learned, last month, that many freelancers share a rarely articulated belief that cold emailing, and even cold network outreach, is largely ineffective. And sometimes these freelancers are cowed into keeping quiet about this belief only because hustling seems to have come to be regarded as a virtue in its own right.

But the overall tenor of these meetings has been positive and encouraging — if for no other reason than that it is at least always nice to connect with another English-speaking freelancer located somewhere else entirely and find that they share largely the same set of aspirations and frustrations as I do. It's opened my eyes to the fact that, once one untethers from a physical workplace and can make freelancing 'work', that person is often also officially location-independent with all the possibility that that entails. There's an exciting world full of adventure waiting to be explored, although, at the same time, I've detected a vague sense of dis-ease with every freelancer I've spoken to who has been 'on the road' for a protracted period of time — so I suspect that a balance between the excitement of travel and the security of a home base is probably the optimal set of conditions (and doubt that an abundance of Zoom calls and Slack channels can ever provide a solution for human's natural instinct to seek affinity in a real-world community — or upend the history of human civilization and return us to a nomadic period, just this time with laptops and smartphones in tow). Although perhaps I'm under-appreciating the extent of the change that is emerging before our very eyes.

For these reasons and more — although reducing meeting bloat seems to have been the flavor of the day in the corporate world for many years — I think that many of us working remotely should be aiming to trend towards *more* interactions with loose, but collaborative, ends rather than less. And as the ranks of those freelancing swells, finding a peer group with similar career aspirations and interests should, theoretically, become easier — it's just that the water cooler around which these newfound communities congregate might be a virtual one, like a Slack workspace, rather than ensconced within an office.

Oddly, I see a sort of distant parallel at play here between the concept of open source in the world of software development — another topic about which I am passionate about and which I will be touching upon in this text.

Some of the difficulties inherent in the freelance lifestyle are well known. For the intended readership, these likely do not require elucidation. And if a continued large scale migration towards remote working and freelancing is going to happen, as anticipated, then these are going to remain open agenda items for resolution.

I believe that those issues can be overcome to a significant extent by being more generous and opening up more when we share information with one another. By being vulnerable enough to let others inspect the codebase upon which the wheels of our businesses turn, so to speak. And by affording them the opportunity to leave comments and suggestions in what, done right, can become an iterative loop of continuous improvement. Call it peer-to-peer collaboration, call it untraditional networking, call it whatever you like. But the process, when done right, can be both symbiotic and self-perpetuating. Not to mention a powerful catalyst for growth.

In order for it to work as well as it can, however, participants need to be relentlessly authentic and open — forthcoming and honest in the information they share about what has been working for them and what hasn't. But they also need to be mindfully tactful when advising others seeking counsel through their struggles or looking for constructive advice to improve (the reticence with which people approached discussing their experience with email marketing underscored this particular point for me).

This also holds true when it comes to opening up conversations about the sometimes hush-hush aspects of freelancing such as the mental health challenges that isolated self-employment carries an inherent risk of posing — both those at the serious end of the spectrum (diagnosable conditions such as anxiety and depression) and those which could be regarded as more 'mild': that collection of day-to-day stresses, anxieties, and frustrations that having a fluctuating income is quite likely to engender. And the former risk is very real. Some studies have found that freelancers are almost twice as likely to be suffering from depression compared to the general population — but I suspect that community support, to lessen the feeling of isolation, could be at least partially helpful in alleviating that trend. Freelancing can be a difficult path to tread — as both anecdotal evidence and the survey findings regarding mental health bear out. But like all paths it is better worn in the company of others. And the bugs inherent in it as a system are, at this stage, well-documented: and that is always the first step in the journey towards resolution.

I hope that the information contained here proves to be of some value to you.

And I wish you much success as you join the freelancing community.

ABOUT THE AUTHOR

Daniel Rosehill (BCL, MA) is a writer based in Jerusalem specializing in providing ghostwriting services for technology clients and — less often — those in the world of public affairs. Daniel previously managed marketing communications (MarCom) at two high-growth technology companies, worked at a PR company, and founded and sold an Irish university news website which grew to be one of the most popular student news sites in the country. His interests include Linux and open source, multimonitor computing, workstation ergonomics, backup solutions, and disaster recovery. Originally from Ireland, Daniel holds an undergraduate degree in Law (BCL) from University College Cork as well as a Master's degree in Journalism (Political) from City University, London. Besides Daniel's writing for clients he has contributed articles to a number of websites and print publications including IrishCentral.com, Geopolitical Monitor, and, several others. In his spare time, Daniel is passionate about languages, exploring world cultures, cooking ethnic cuisines, entrepreneurship, travel, computers, and (yes, really) collecting national flags. But mostly he is just passionate about learning.

KNOWLEDGE MENU (Table of Contents)

INTRODUCTION

Countless people around the world these days are looking towards freelancing as a means of boosting their primary income — or providing one in its entirety.

Whether transitioning into freelancing from scratch, or gradually scaling up a 'side hustle,' there is a lot to be mastered at once in order to become a successful freelancer or small business owner.

For one, exemplary skills should be a prerequisite for most. Whether you're looking to succeed as a freelance writer, as a graphic designer, as an independent architect, or as a Java programmer, it helps to be good — or if possible *superlatively* good — at whatever professional service it is that you intend charging future clients for.

Business connections are also vitally important in the freelance world. In fact, no matter how loud the "*hustle harder*" drumbeat roars, the extent to which tapping into the value of pre-existing long-term relationships matters remains, in my opinion, grossly underappreciated. Although, in a sense, that is nothing new under the sun. Freelancing has always been a hotly competitive marketplace. But freelancers these days compete (in a sense) on a worldwide scale for business against one another. This is something which gig economy marketplaces, such as Upwork, have arguably exploited to freelancers' detriment — by pitting those with grossly unequal living costs directly against one another in a race, for buyers, to the bottom. Unsurprisingly, this has had a chilling effect on the rates freelancers who sell their offerings on these marketplaces can command. But *if* this is true (that the freelance marketplace is truly global — and I include 'if' because there are some instances in which it can be argued that it is not), then it has perhaps never been more so than at the turbulent time when this text is being written — a point in time when low barriers to entry and an influx into the gig economy of those who have, unfortunately, lost their jobs meet at a confluence. And it's a confluence which, at least in the short term, is likely to create a glut on the supply side of that market — with the usual effect on pricing that the law of supply and demand dictates will occur.

Escaping that dynamic unscathed represents perhaps the central challenge for those entering the freelance marketplace for the first time right now. Inbound marketing strategies, cold email pitching, and applying for "gigs" certainly all have their role to play in today's freelancers' hustling arsenal (and it is an arsenal that needs to be continuously honed and perfected to have best effect) but increasingly these tools are going to have to be used intelligently to yield good effect. Having a pre-established network of professional contacts ready to refer on work when you need it is therefore a massive strategic advantage — if for no other reason than it gives you breathing space while you get all the other pieces of the puzzle in place and well oiled (and assembling that puzzle is the subject matter of this book.) If these dynamics all sound unfavorable towards freelancers, however, then you should be relieved to know that is not necessarily the case. There are premium marketplaces and clients looking for premium services just as there are those looking for cheap deals — unfortunately the former just aren't quite as easy to pin down with a Google search as Upwork is. But those that want to enter this market need to do everything in their power to stand out from the competition.

So assuming that you already have all the basic prerequisites mentioned at the start of this chapter in place (namely, the skills to freelance and possibly a couple of first clients culled from your existing network), the small matter of the technology you will need to equip yourself with to maintain and ultimately scale your business then looms large for many. While operating robust technology isn't likely to represent your golden ticket to freelance largesse, doing things like sending your introduction from a branded email address, and your invoices from a professional invoice management platform, can all help distinguish you as a serious professional rather than somebody casually sidelining in whatever service you are providing.

There are obvious things to help achieve this which one might feel barely merit mention but which will be covered here for the sake of being thorough and starting, truly, from first freelancing principles. What does a good internet service look like might be one of them? Do I need hosting for my website might be another? We will also look at ones that are more likely to give pause for thought. Most freelancers — most denizens of the earth, in fact, I would venture to say — have likely heard about the cloud at some point or another. But what, exactly, is the cloud, you might have wondered? Is it up there somewhere in orbit with the International Space Station? What should you have up there (or it down there)? Perhaps a CRM, like Salesforce or Hubspot, you might be wondering? You might have seen people waxing lyrical about them in a Facebook group and had your interest piqued (and by the way, there's a whole world of those waiting for you to explore if you're not already doing that!). But *what's* a CRM, you may ask? After learning about what it does (SaaS; chapter four) you may still decide to do without one, at least initially. Maybe you reckon you'll manage hand-crafting those crucial pitch emails one-by-one — and if you're doing so in small volume, that's a valid approach to take. But either way you'll want to make a professional impression. How, you might be wondering, can you get one of those fancy-looking vanity email addresses that don't end in Gmail.com (basic web infrastructure; chapter three)? All these points, and other ones, will be covered in the forthcoming chapters.

For many freelancers, the whole realm of technology is perceived to be a minefield that they are happy to defer wading into for as long as possible — or to delegate the process of poking through its crooks and crannies and deciphering its sometimes bewildering jargon to a misfortune and more youthful relative. In many cases the person cast into the hapless role of I.T.-Manager-by-Proxy might be a child under your roof — somebody that can be commandeered into the effort while they are still in high school, if even just periodically.

Like with most difficult things in life, however, when it comes to getting to grips with technology avoidance is not usually the best long-term strategy — and as a sometimes adult-child-helper to intermittently technically-stricken family members, I will happily and strongly assert that relying upon your children to be available to remind you how to log in to Wordpress (when they are busy with other things!) is *not* always a practical strategy. (Potential tech-savvy children that have not yet been recruited to the cause: take it from me that autonomous skill-development is the only answer to your parents' technical quandaries— no amount of documentation you can cobble together will ever be enough!) There's also an awful lot to keep on top of when it comes to technology these days. You could say that trying to keep up to date with technology these days is like trying to keep a fast moving target in frame. And it's arguably never been moving faster than it is right now. But that also, oddly, makes it a good time at which to start.

The purpose of this short guide — available in both ebook and paperback format on Amazon.com — is to equip freelancers with the basic concepts and know-how they might need in order to better optimize their technology 'stack.' The freelancer-centricity of these recommendations will usually be limited to their scale (small) as well as the typical collection of technical tools which freelancers often feel that they require to succeed in the marketplace.

Beyond that, we'll look at the various technologies that are out there and which you *might* be interested in using in your freelance business. And I use the word 'might' advisedly because, when it comes to technology, less is sometimes more. But I still think it's worthwhile to know what layers might be fitting into your stack *before* you start building it. And that's a useful opportunity to get our first piece of jargon out of the way: A 'stack' simply means (roughly) the set of tools and integrations that somebody uses to run a business or handle a key functionality of it such as sales or marketing (or accounting) A 'sales stack,' for instance, might consist of a CRM, a VoIP tool, and a few other tools (perhaps an email finding product)— all working in harmony thanks to the power of integrations, a subject which we will touch upon in the SaaS and cloud computing chapter. It comes from the idea that, in technology, things are often layered one on top of another in order to work: For instance, in order to visit a website, the files and database that might comprise the website need to be hosted somewhere on the internet so that they can be delivered to your computer over it. That person needs to have a technology like Apache running on their webserver in order to be able to drive the website to you (which, in turn, needs to hosted on a compatible operating system, like Ubuntu Server Edition or Debian Server). Naturally, the person hosting the website will also need access to some infrastructure with computing power upon which the aforementioned applications can live. In this example, that infrastructure will probably be a server in a data center somewhere (web hosting; chapter three). And, in all likelihood, that person is running a combination of software tools on that server in order to help deliver an engaging website to you. And that might contain a mixture of both dynamic and static content (Wordpress would be a good example). In this day and age they are probably also leveraging the power of third-party scripts, like Google Analytics, which they have injected dynamically into the site's pages in order to learn more about who you are and how you are interacting with the website they operate. This isn't as privacy-invasive as it might, at first glance, sound: in all likelihood their intentions here are purely selfish and centered around trying to gain information that will help them improve their website and make it more interesting for future browsers. And their ultimate end, in that endeavor, might be to get more people to place an order (ecommerce) or to get more people to book meetings using a Calendly embed. But to do that they will need to know what pages you are visiting, how long you spend on each page, and what page you leave their website at. It could be said, therefore, that the simple act of visiting a website relies on there being many more things operating 'under the hood' than might meet the eye at first glance — or even which might meet the eye by opening Developer Tools and peering a little deeper into the code which the website has served up to your browser. In this case, an entire 'stack' of hardware and software components was required to simply ensure that somebody can operate a website which somebody else, such as you, can sit down at an internet-computer with an installed web browser and access.

This book was written with the type of freelancer in mind who — when confronted with the question of which hosting plan to buy, possibly his or her first major business technology decision — is likely to throw up their hands in exasperation and reach for some variation of "*me, I'm a writer — I should go ask a techie that!*"

While this book should certainly equip you with the principles and basic know-how I have outlined above, equally this book will not tell you *everything* that there is to know about technology.

That journey, if you were to embark upon it with any measure of diligence, would require a couple of advanced university degrees, countless certifications (some specific to technologies, others specific to vendors), and an awful lot of hands-on playing around with things like Artificial Intelligence (AI) algorithms and the other emerging technology that represents the leading edge of today's market. In fact, I doubt that such a journey would be possible in your average human lifetime — not to mention the fact that a good chunk of the knowledge you learn would become deprecated as you acquire it and other lacunae in your knowledge would simultaneously open up as new technologies come to market to replace the deprecated ones in the iterative process of refinement and replacement that we simply refer to as 'advancement'. Therefore, a more viable strategy is to focus on a narrow sliver of the technology in existence in the world — and to look, in particular, at that which stands the best chance of improving your life in an appreciable way. This book follows that process — and looks at the technologies which an average freelancer might expect to want to understand.

The presentation of topics offered here might also, at first glance, seem somewhat non-linear. This text will skip over some straightforward things that I think you are better off understanding, or becoming acquainted with, by reading user manuals or (let's be realistic here!) running a quick Google search. In that category might be questions such as how to install desktop word processing software if that's something that you still use (and here I must point out: even Microsoft has put out some excellent online processors these days). But it *should* give you a well-rounded understanding of the types of systems that you may wish to deploy to get your freelance business off on a good footing — and to streamline the journey towards scalability, growth, and success once you've got there. It might even, as the subtitle suggests, give you the information that you'll need in order to *be* your very own IT department — at least during your freelance business's founding years but perhaps even indefinitely.

Who am I to dole out all this self-proclaimed tech wisdom, you may be wondering?

My name is Daniel Rosehill. I'm a writer — possibly just like you are — who specializes in writing about technology. I've spent the best part of the last ten years involved in writing and communications to greater or lesser extents— more latterly at technology startups, a PR company, and these days for my own business which I must humbly suggest that you use for *all* your *marketing technical writing* needs (sadly, I haven't yet figured out a way to get my brain to enjoy writing API documentation).

Everybody, it seems, has their peculiar interests within technology. Mine, which I'll flag here at the outset, are Linux and open source. Although I promise that I'll try not to convince you that you need to trick out your home office with a Linux desktop, I *will* point out the potential benefits of open source and self-hosted alternatives to the more fashionable and commonly used breed of software as a service (SaaS) cloud software. I'll try to do this only when I truly believe that viable alternatives exist that may be worthy of your valued consideration.

There are other ways in which this won't be a particularly traditional primer on technology (to the extent, that is, that those exist). I'll include topics that few like to spend time thinking about — the supreme importance of having a great backup regiment being one I am keen to drive home — simply because I feel, in earnest, that having that knowledge is important to have from the get-to. Even, yes, when you're a one person band — and even when a laptop and a Gmail account together might represent the totality of the technical infrastructure that you may be interested in protecting. And I'll jump over other topics entirely— besides installing desktop software, enterprise user directory management, for instance — because they don't apply at the freelancer level of scale (unless you're going to skyrocket to tycoon level *really* quickly, and you can probably employ a real I.T. person to set up hundreds of workstations when that happens).

I'll also mention a couple more things that you almost certainly *don't* need to know right now, or maybe ever, but which I think that you *should* anyway just because I feel like they are truly awesome things to know about (let's put UPSs, which are like mini backup power sources, in that category). When the power goes out just as you're about to finish that article but you can keep hammering at the keyboard you will thank me.

And that's really the critical factor which determines freelancing success, in my opinion: Drinking copious amounts of coffee and hammering furiously at a keyboard for about 12 hours a day, at least, until you wake up one morning and figure out that you have enough paying clients to sustain your lifestyle and are sort of — somehow! — making it all work.

Just kidding (well, sort of).

Much success with whatever it is that you do.

Now let's take a look at the technology you might want to arm yourself with in order to get there.

1. GETTING CONNECTED

Because it's hard to achieve much these days without an internet connection

Whatever it is that you're planning on freelancing in, I believe it is fairly safe to assume these days that you're planning on doing it online — at least in part.

If you weren't then I'm guessing that you wouldn't have much interest in a book about technology for freelancers. And if you *are* a bricks and mortar only freelancer (I'm aware that they still exist!) then I suggest that you look into whether e-commerce could give you access to international markets — and boost your bottom line. In many cases, it's a viable option. And at the very least having a strong web presence with which to market yourself makes a lot of sense if you want to take your marketing beyond word of mouth and get your message out to people in far-flung corners of the world.

When it boils down to it there are only two major prerequisites to achieving online connectivity — the equipment you'll need to get connected to the internet and the provision of a service for internet connectivity. I'm sorry to have to start things off on what for some might be an overly simplistic footing, but getting connected to the internet is where many a freelancer's technology planning starts. In this chapter, let's take a look at both of these things — getting an internet connection and equipping yourself with a computer — in turn.

The Internet

It's hard to describe what the internet is without coming very close to plagiarizing the Wikpedia entry on the subject. And I'm doing this aware that you almost undoubtedly *understand* what it does simply from time spent using it.

The internet is a massive worldwide system of interconnected computers. And those computers communicate with one another over a defined protocol suite called TCP/IP for exchanging information. In fact, you'll probably want to own (or lease) one of each type of computer that the internet is comprised of even just as a freelancer: a desktop or laptop with which to *consume* the internet (receive and view its pages) and a server, in the cloud somewhere, with which to host and *serve* an internet website for other people with desktops or laptops to view (or programatically – to send your content or program data to other servers). In fact, from a strict conceptual standpoint, there's really no difference between a desktop, a laptop, and a server other than the ease with which your typical user can interface with them. They're all internet-connected storage repositories capable of transmitting (uploading) and receiving (downloading) packets of information. We'll see that later when we go about installing some things in the cloud.

So how do you get in on the fun, you may be wondering?

You'll firstly need a computer which has the ability to interface with the internet through a networking card. And unless you happen to be involved in buying computer supplies for an ultra-secure critical infrastructure project that needs to be detached from the internet entirely (in cybersecurity, this concept is called 'air gapping' and is still used), then you can safely assume that whatever computing device you've purchased has this capability. Most likely it has both a port for you to stick in ethernet cabling and receive wired internet directly from your router as well as a card for connecting to wireless internet (WiFi, which is shorthand for wireless internet connectivity based upon the Institute of Electrical and Electronics Engineer's 802.2 protocol). We'll take a cursory look at what you might want to look for in the type of laptop or desktop you need later in this chapter when we cover hardware and software components. But first, let's get ourselves connected to a viable internet connection.

Choosing an ISP

In practice, there are two ways for anybody to get online connectivity at home or in an office these days: pay for a dedicated internet connection or attempt to simply utilize the internet data connection that you almost undoubtedly have as part of your smartphone subscription.

The first model entails paying a monthly subscription fee to an internet service provider — which is known, as the acronym those words creates goes, simply as an ISP. And the internet service provider will typically sell you a package. This package defines a few parameters for the internet connection that you can access: what kind of speed you will be able to achieve and (in some cases) how much internet you can use every month. The latter is known as bandwidth. Like with many service offerings, ISPs typically offer various subscription tiers with the higher priced tiers offering better features. Common add-on products include a static IP address (otherwise, you can expect your public IP address — which identifies the source of your traffic — to regularly change. This could be problematic if you are set up to have access to services based on your connecting IP.)

There are other qualitative differences you're likely to encounter when trying to choose between competitors. For example, some providers are able to transmit internet over high speed fiber optic cable. While others use DSL and others still use simple cable. The difference between the type of cable used by your ISP to deliver its infrastructure matters only insofar as that it allows for internet connections of very different speed to be provisioned to home users.

Among the most crucial aspects you'll want to evaluate when selecting an ISP will be the connection speed that the ISP promises to deliver. And there are two speeds that you'll want to take a look at: the upload speed and the download speed (even though only one, the download speed, will typically feature prominently in your ISP's advertising collateral). Both are measured, these days, in megabits per second — which is denoted Mbps (just to clarify: MBps — with an upper case 'B' — refers to mega*bytes* per second. This is commonly used to measure file data transfer speeds rather than internet connections). One important to thing to note: it's important to read the fine print — always, but particularly when buying an internet connection and committing yourself to a contract for its supply. Many ISPs will guarantee your connection speed *"up to"* the package that you have subscribed to — but not set a floor or a minimum beneath which your connection speed will be deemed unacceptable. For instance, if you're paying for a plan that is supposed to deliver 100 Mbps connectivity but frequently experience an internet connection that compares, unfavorably, with the dial-up internet era — and you raise the issue, in ire, with your ISP — you might find, quite exasperatingly, that your ISP argues back that your lousy and virtually unusable 5 Mbps connection is *"within the terms of our contract - your plan gives you up to 100 Mbps."* The operative terminology here, of course, is 'up to' — and these two little words have resulted in much frustration for many unhappy internet customers. Beyond verbal trickery of that nature, the nuances of what each ISP can offer vary a little depending on the regulatory framework at play in the jurisdiction within which they are offered. But it's important, again, that you scrutinize the fine print and don't be afraid to pose hard questions to slick internet salespeople whose primary motivation might be to make a commission from a quick sale.

Of the two speeds we discussed one is likely to be of supreme importance to you. Your download speed is the speed that most people think about when they ask *"how fast"* an internet connection is. It's called a *"down*load" speed because it's the speed at which data (like IP packets) travels *from* servers to your computer. Conversely, the *up*load speed is the speed at which data moves from a machine on your Local Area Network (LAN) *up* to "the internet" — the Wide Area Network (WAN) which exists beyond the point in the wall where your router receives cabling that taps it into the broader network with which your computer interfaces whenever it browses websites. Lest you think that the upload speed doesn't matter — it certainly does. But its speed, in relation to the downlink, can vary quite considerably. Here's a screenshot from a speed test of a typical residential internet connection to illustrate the point.

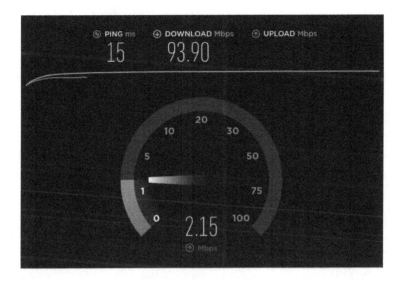

As you can see, the upload speed, which was in the process of being measured when this screenshot was taken, is very small in comparison to the download number that this connection is posting (the connection's latency, how quickly it reaches the test server, is measured by the ping metric in milliseconds.)

How much the strength (or weakness) of the upload speed which a package promises to provide matters depends on what you're likely to be *doing* online. You "upload" data to the internet, for instance, whenever you:

- Create an album on Facebook by sending photos to the social network for inclusion;
- Upload a video to YouTube;
- Push a backup to a server in the cloud;
- Host a website and serve its contents to those that have expressed an interest in viewing it by navigating to its URL (as we'll discuss in the hosting chapter it is usually

possible to host your own sites at home, although in practice this approach is not very advisable)

The kicker here is that the amount of data involved in each of these cases varies *considerably* — massively, in fact, might be a better word. While adding a Facebook album from your first freelanceversary (remember the word!) might constitute moving a few megabytes worth of files up to Facebook's Content Delivery Network (CDN) — and can be done reasonably quickly at just about *any* upload speed above dial-up— uploading a full disk image of your hard drive might mean trying to move an archive with terabytes of data from your computer to a remote server. And unless you have a strong enough upload connection, that process could conceivably take days or even weeks of tedious uploading. (We'll take a look at offsite backups in chapter five; in the meantime, know that there are calculators online if you ever need to estimate how long a particular upload/download operation might be expected to take).

As you may have noticed from the above screenshot, many residential internet connections are heavily biased towards the download side. And that's because regular internet users do *not* tend to be in the habit of doing elaborate things like uploading full drive backups to the cloud — so it's a part of the service that ISPs do not have to deliver on all that well (or rather they just have to deliver a good enough upload speed that it doesn't take infuriatingly long to upload some photos to Facebook). If you're just a casual internet user, then one of these connections is probably all that you will ever need to enjoy many happy and productive days spent on the internet earning yourself a living as a freelancer. However, if you really need a fixed upload speed or a Service Level Agreement (SLA) that is robust enough not to include any room for verbal ambiguity of the like

I described then you should know that there are options for you too.

What we've been looking at so far, in bare detail, is the world of residential internet connectivity — which is typically purchased from a consumer-facing ISP (these are usually well-known companies and often sell internet as bundles alongside television subscription services). But there's a whole different universe out there for those whose internet connectivity needs are comparable to the serious players of industry. And that's 'business internet'. It's worth pointing out that the exactly terminology which delineates between 'residential' and 'commerical-standard' internet isn't controlled or defined — so you should be able to take 'commercial grade internet' or something similar into Google and dredge up a list of providers in your locality.

Some of the companies that offer business internet will offer a specific type of subscription called Dedicated Internet Access (DIA). These packages — in theory — offer consumers a guaranteed provision of internet resources by reserving bandwidth from the provider's network for each user that purchases the package. The Service Level Agreements (SLA) which a commercial ISP offers these consumers is often much more exacting than the sort of nebulous *"up to"* verbiage which many ordinary residential consumers receive (if they can be bothered to read their fine print and find out what they are supposed to be getting, that is — and I will admit that, like many, I have often discovered the limits of what I had signed up to only by hearing it read back to my by my ISP's technical support!). In the majority of cases, freelancers and small business owners will (more than) suffice with a standard residential connection. But in the event that a use-case arises which calls for a reliable uplink of, say, 100 Mbps, business grade internet might be the place to start looking if residential connections offering such a guaranteed connection speed cannot be easily procured.

Getting Physically Connected: Routers and Networks

Once you've decided upon a provider and a package, a technician from your ISP will usually come to your home, or your office, bearing with them a tremendous hardware device called a router (so called because it contains a 'switch' to route traffic internally as well a modem to connect you to the network beyond your home or office — which, as we mentioned, we can simply denote as the 'internet').

As I just mentioned, the 'router' is actually a router and a modem which are combined, these days, into the once piece of hardware (remember those funny things that plugged into the wall and made squeaky sounds when you connected to the internet? They haven't been entirely deprecated — they've just evolved). The router will allow you to set up a local area network (LAN) by plugging ethernet cables tethered on the other end to computers into its LAN slots. But more importantly (because you probably didn't sign up for internet so that you could share files between your laptop and a desktop), it also allows each device on the LAN to connect to the all-important 'internet' — which we described as the globally interconnected IP-based network which sits beyond our local network. The internet can be accessed, by the user, from a variety of graphical frontends but the most common of these — and the one which, some experts say, will one day constitute the only frontend — is a web browser. Google Chrome and Mozilla Firefox are common examples. (If like me, you find intriguing the idea that one day operating systems and desktop software will become largely obsolete and everybody will simply connect to the internet from a very pared down computer with a browser, then look up the concept of thin computing. Sadly, it's never quite taken off. But what the future will bring — who knows!)

Once you have provisioned internet connectivity in your workplace or place of residence, connecting to the network is extremely straightforward. Personally, I'm a big fan of plugging my (desktop) directly into the router using ethernet (RJ45) cabling. This generally gives a faster and more reliable connection than connecting to the internet over the air (WiFi). That's because the strength of a WiFi signal depends upon how close one is to the transmitter as well as other factors such as the amount of concrete intervening between where the router sits and where you are trying to connect from. Ethernet cabling, at reasonable lengths, essentially provides the internet connection that is being cabled into your home. And one quick point about that. If you're joining the Luddite bandwagon with me by using ethernet, then I advise that you avoid the temptation, if you feel one that is, to skimp on ethernet cabling: various grades and standards actually guarantee different maximum speeds. And you never know when your ISP will come knocking at your door offering you super high speed fiber optic connectivity. When they do, you'll want to make sure that you have your CAT 7a cable on hand so that you can take advantage of every megabyte of the full speed that the connection offers and get those terabyte backups flying up to the cloud in time for tea.

In some cases, you can install your own router in place of the one that your ISP issued. If you do that you can then load your own firmware onto it if it doesn't already come preinstalled. Often, if you do this, you will get a much more powerful router than the one your ISP provided. This isn't because your ISP wants to equip you with a lousy piece of hardware: it's simply a reflection of the fact that most people don't want to do sophisticated things with their home network and something caused by the business model they operate. ISPs are often in the business of supplying internet connectivity to hundreds of thousands of customers. They tend to buy, in enormous quantities, routers that "just work" in order to supply them to their customers — and periodically offer them for replacement another 'safe bet' router in a few years' time. Needless to say, these are not necessarily the same routers that deliver the most cutting edge set of features. There's another reason why buying your own router might be a technical boon. Open source router firmware, such as Tomato, OpenWrt, and DD-WRRT, give you more leeway to change configuration settings than the default options which your ISP may have locked down. There are downsides to be aware of too, however. You may find, for instance, that you have lost the ability to badger your ISP's technical support people with all your support questions when things go awry as they are bound to from time to time. You might also find that your ISP's support people are now unequipped to remotely access its settings and conduct diagnostics. Bridging between your ISP-issued router and a router of your choosing is a final configuration option which some choose to deploy. This typically uses point to point ethernet to bring the internet connection across between the two routers (bridging) and then serves it from the secondary device whose configuration can be more easily modified. But the use cases for when this makes sense are relatively marginal. In all likelihood the only other things you'll likely need to know about your router beyond verifying whether it's turned on or off (and remember: the turn on turn off toggle maneuver is your all time top troubleshooting move!) are:

- **How to install a VPN onto it**, if you chose to do so that is. If you install a VPN on your router than all devices connected to it — whether they are connected over WiFi or ethernet — will inherit the VPN tunnel and connect to the internet through it. Commercial VPN companies usually set some ceiling for the number of devices that can be simultaneously connected even on a paid subscription. For this reason, if you have a lot of devices at home, and want them all to connect to the internet over a VPN, finding one that can install on the router makes the most sense.

- **How to change the default DNS settings** so that they inherit across the local network. We'll look at the Domain Name System (DNS) in more detail later — but, in brief, it's the system that converts from alphanumeric URLs to public IP addresses to help you access websites with ease. Your ISP will, by default, have set up the router it provided to use the DNS servers that it uses for its customers (these may be ones that it also operates). However, there are third party DNS resolving networks such as OpenDNS and Google Public DNS which might do a better job. OpenDNS, for instance, expands the typical functionalities provided by DNS: not only might it allow you to resolve DNS queries more quickly, thus speeding up your browsing experience, it will also allow you to configure parental control settings. The DNS settings on your router (even the one your ISP provides) can usually be quite easily changed by accessing an embedded web server which allows you to manipulate its settings. The address for this embedded web server is typically displayed on a printed sticker on the back of your router. Anybody that can connect to your internet network can have access. As the default login credentials are often 'admin' (username) and 'admin' (password) it is highly recommended that you change at least one of these credentials.

- **How to set up port forwarding** if you want to access a network device, such as a local server, from beyond the home network. Again, the use case for hosting websites on your home network is fairly marginal. But we'll cover it in the chapter on website hosting nevertheless.

Option Two: Mobile-Only Internet Connectivity

The second option I'll present for internet connectivity — and one which is especially popular among digital nomads — is to use an internet hotspot and simply use the data plan that your mobile network operator (MNO) has provided. These days, the cost of connectivity in all forms is plummeting. And many providers of cellphone services, in a bid to woo you from their competitors, are in the habit of offering a far higher monthly data limit than most users will ever require by doing normal things with their cellphone. In other instances, there's no data cap at all — and instead the amount of data you can have access to, without being charged extra or throttled that is, is governed by the provisions of fair usage terms usually buried well into the fine print of your contract (a similar concept applies to webhosts that offer "unlimited" resources).

I've already disclosed that I'm a Linux fan and use a desktop rather than a laptop. Therefore, it should come as no surprise to learn that I prefer the idea of simply having my computer tethered physically to my local network and using that for connectivity. And I prefer to use a proper home network for connectivity along the lines of the one I described in the previous chapter. Using an internet hotspot is fine as a temporary solution — I spent a couple of weeks working from one while waiting to get internet in a new apartment and, although the speed wasn't ideal, it mostly worked out. There are providers of international SIM cards that can offer you a contract with fixed data internationally. These data-only SIMs are ideal when used in conjunction with a 4G router. But — if you plan on working from home, whether substantially or fully, and doing so from the same physical location rather than moving about the world — an excellent internet connection, along the lines I described earlier, is a far more pragmatic option and usually more than worth the monthly subscription fee.

There's one thing that you can do involving cellular data, which I *do* recommend, however.

Cellular routers — such as 4G routers — are becoming increasingly commonplace and relatively inexpensive. If, like me, you take your business continuity quite seriously, then you might want to invest in an extra data SIM just to have something to run off if the internet goes down *without* having to power up your cellphone's hotspot. Likewise if you're on the road a lot: having to tether data from your cellphone is not the best long-term strategy and will likely quickly exhaust its battery life. If you're deploying a secondary router simply for backup purposes then this is really "going the extra mile" preparedness-wise (even having two internet connections, one only as a backup option, isn't unheard of and the same thing could be said about it). In most cases, however, *one* good ISP-provided home internet connection is all that you will need to get happily surfing and stay that way for as long as you are in contract.

Making The Final ISP Decision

One final tip on the ISP front before we move on to the interface you'll need to connect to the wonderful network of websites which this technology gives you convenient and round-the-clock access to.

In any technology vertical saturated with options (antivirus and VPN markets are particularly noteworthy examples) marketing can be expected to be fierce — even bewildering to the average consumer at times.

As I have tried to delineate above, there *are* a few features which distinguish different internet connections objectively and qualitatively from one another. Things which can be determined by asking simple questions to those trying to sell you the solutions in order to quickly cut through the noise. Questions like:

- What is the download speed which this plan offers? What is the upload speed?
- Is there a minimum threshold that is guaranteed with either?
- Is there a bandwidth cap which I'm reasonably likely to surpass with expected usage?
- How much does it cost?
- If I want to cancel, how easily can I do so?

A lot the information provided beyond this simply runs the risk of creating needless confusion in the minds of consumers.

When it comes to ISPs at least, it's also worth knowing that geography *does* matter. Because different ISPs sometimes deliver internet from different underlying infrastructure — the quality of which can be *very* location-sensitive — it's worth asking around in your neighborhood if some basic pricing research hasn't yielded a definitive 'winner' in your evaluation of which is the best option for your particular use-case.

You might, for instance, start by trying to find out

- What connection does your neighbor have?
- Is it consistently good?
- How about during weekends and at night: are there noticeable slowdowns?
- How is the customer service if things go wrong?
- How long, on average, does it take to get a technician out?

These are all questions which you might be able to get more objective and fair answers to by knocking on your neighbor's door rather than by searching on Google. But, for the sake of being thorough, why not do both. A freelancer who trod the digital nomad path for a number of years once told me that it has now become commonplace to ask prospective Airbnb hosts to take a speed test screenshot to demonstrate the strength of the internet connection which those staying at the property might be able to expect. Clearly, a reliable and speedy internet connection is an extremely valuable commodity in the life of a freelance writer. Find a good one and stick with it. You — and any digital nomad guests you host — will be happy that you did.

Getting A Computer

As a freelancer, you're going to be spending an inordinate amount of time pecking away at a keyboard and moving a mouse around a screen while cursing the fact that your latest client is now 50 days late on his invoice.

Trust me on this one.

If someone told you that this gig is easy, you're probably going to be eating your words by the time you're finished reading this book.

Freelancers, by and large, tend to work inordinately long hours — often far in excess of the forty hour week that is typical across much of the developed world. FreelancerMap.com pegged the average figure at 47 hours per week. Although many freelancers I know routinely put in a hefty multiple of that. Is the four hour work week a worthy aspiration? Absolutely. Should you strive towards working smarter rather than harder? Also. But setting realistic expectations for your initial time in business is a good way to avoid subsequent disappointment.

Ergonomics Matter A Lot

If you asked your average cubicle worker to describe what mental picture arises when he/she hears the word 'freelancer,' I would be willing to bet five meters of my finest CAT7 ethernet cabling that they would firstly picture an individual in his or her pajamas — at an hour, needless to say, when pajamas are not the expected home office attire. That individual would furthermore probably be sprawled out in bed. And — just for added patheticness — hunched over a laptop (if they're even using that!) typing keystrokes with one hand and clutching a bowel of breakfast cereal with the other.

Again, let me put my contrarian credentials on full show here.

As I've mentioned, I use a desktop. Yes, those old-school things that plug into the wall and stay there. The only time I use my laptop computer is when I'm attending in-person meetings or traveling. If I'm doing neither of those things, then months can sometimes elapse without the device being powered on. Far be it from me to hold myself out as some paragon of freelance productivity, but I do not believe that I have completed any project work in bed — at least during the past few years. (About the pajamas .... to maintain the professional image I'm trying so hard to project let's not mention what I do about my outfit for now!)

I'm building towards a point here.

If you're putting in long and grueling hours — and in all likelihood you *will* be as a freelancer, at least initially— then it's worth thinking about ergonomics: the physical contours and comfort level of the tools which will help sustain the processes you'll need to be comfortable and successful. Closely allied to the concept of workplace ergonomics is the idea of human factors — simply put, the fact that you are a human with human needs and not a mechanical factor of production — and both, ideally, need to be addressed. But making suggestions about how to create a good home office is easier than trying to coach you through how to be at your happiest as a freelancer (something I am unqualified to do). So let's leave our treatment of this topic to just the former.

And ergonomics are undoubtedly vital. Without doing the above (working from a well designed home office and at an optimally configured desktop-based workstation) I think there's a good chance I would be a hunch-back by now. That's because put simply laptops are (without modification) *not* designed to be used ergonomically for any protracted period of time. Desktop computers, in comparison, can be carefully arranged to ensure that they *are* the centerpieces around which ergonomically-sound workstations revolve. And if you're thinking about going down the desktop route (friendly word of warning: you can get into them enough that it can become a wallet-depleting rabbit hole!), then you'll probably want to have a laptop on hand as well for those times when you *do* leave the comfort of your home base. (Friendly word of advice part two: if you *are* working from home try to ensure that this happens at least daily!). The key words above are 'without modification'. A variety of mobile devices *can* be successfully worked with in a way that yields an acceptable degree of ergonomics (and by 'acceptable' I mean acceptable for your body). Beyond the majority of freelancers who work primarily from laptops, there are even some news stringers and field-ruggedized reporters-turned-freelance-writers whose preferred *modus operandi* is to input copy into a smartphone or tablet using a Bluetooth keyboard. For many, having both a good quality mobile and stationary device might be the best course of action — but if you're going down that route some thought is always required to think how it can best be used for the duration of an entire (and long) workweek.

I'm not here to judge anybody's working style — even though that's clearly what I'm doing. But I *am* saying that if you're going to be working one way for a long period of time it makes sense to think about how comfortable that working environment is to your body. The damage caused by things like poor posture and straining your neck awkwardly could accrue quite significantly over time. The long hours that the freelancing journey poses might compound the effect and accelerate any untoward dynamics caused by a poorly planned workstation — such that one gets sorer quicker than an office worker who might have coworkers and a less desk-centric workday to ensure that he/she periodically gets up for some leg-stretching. While a desktop workstation allows you free reign to set up peripherals at the best height and position to suit your body, laptops and other devices can also be configured in this manner — it just takes a little more maneuvering and a few more accessories. If you're intent on using a laptop full-time then, at a minimum, consider using an external monitor so that you're not squinting downwards while straining your neck and trying to make out whether that invoice is overdue by 50 days or by 51. Using a mouse is better than contorting your hands to flit back and forth to a trackpad. An external keyboard can also be helpful — and given how affordable basic peripherals have become a wireless keyboard/mouse combination kit could easily be left at every locale where one has a frequently used workstation. Finally, docking stations are excellent tools designed for just this purpose: to quickly connect a variety of commonly needed peripherals to an intermittently available laptop.

Configuring The Perfect Workstation

Back to workstation ergonomics. If you look online, you can find calculators which will — based on your height — give you the correct height, as validated by ergonomic research, at which to set your desk and your chair at. This is why — in the most ideal of situations — both one's desk and chair would be adjustable. However, given that minutely adjustable desks cost considerably more than your typical IKEA Linnmon-and-Adlis workstation combo (some call this the 'L&A'), it's worth ensuring, at a minimum, that you purchase an office chair which can move in both directions vertically.

To set up a *basic* ergonomically-compliant workstation you should also:

- **Measure the distance between where you sit and your monitors.** Most sources recommend that the distance should exceed 51 cm.
- **Measure the viewing angle**: how far you have to turn your glance down in order to view the contents of your 'screens'. Many sources recommend that that angle should be about 15 degrees (you should need to shift your gaze about 15 degrees downward in order to comfortably see the contents of your screen — or each of them).

Of course, there's a lot that you can do beyond ensuring that your desk and chair are at the right height, your screens are positioned at the right distance on your desk, and your peripherals are at the right height too (if you want to take this approach then a keyboard tray can be built into a desk). A good chair with adjustable armrests and a full back support that pivots back and forth is very helpful too. But the above should be enough to ensure at least some basic level of ergonomic comfort.

VESA Monitor Arms

In light of the above, there's one piece of kit that I would like to recommend in particular. And those are VESA monitor mounts.

You're probably familiar with monitor mounts. But if not, they're those "arms" holding flatscreen monitors that you've probably seen in the news whenever they reel in stock footage from some investment bank or trading floor just before the stock market crashed. They screw into the backs of monitors at standard configurations. There are two standard VESA hole patterns — 75mm x 75mm and 100mm x 100mm — and these refer to the number of millimeters at which the mounting holes are spaced apart. If you have a monitor that you're intent on using but notice, upon turning it around, that it doesn't have VESA holes, then all hope is not lost. VESA brackets are available for sale on Amazon. They're not the most attractive of solutions but *do* allow you to mount non-VESA monitors on an arm by clasping around the screen from the back. Finally, if you're deploying multiple monitors that are part of an array then ideally these should be of the same make and brand. If you buy multiple units of the exact same monitor then they should all mount perfectly level. Otherwise, even if one uses monitors of the same screen dimension one is likely to find annoying small discrepancies between manufacturers and monitor models caused by minor variations in the height at which the VESA mounts are screwed into the back panel of the monitor. There's another benefit to multiplying the same screen. From a software perspective, you should only need to worry about maintaining one driver. This is advantageous for several reasons and also helps to ensure that your multiple monitors all display a consistent picture from screen to screen.

The advantage of having your monitors on mounts is that — ergonomically — you can easily position them at the most comfortable distance and viewing angle for you, making fine adjustments as you grow comfortable at your workstation within the parameters of the recommendations described above. By contrast, the plastic stand with which most LCD monitors cannot easily be adjusted — either for height or for pivot (that's if you discount shoving disused books under each monitor as a viable adjustment strategy!)

The ergonomic friendliness of VESA monitor brackets holds true for even the most basic entry-level versions (at the time of writing Amazon Basics includes very affordable options for both single and dual monitor mounts). Pricier articulating mounts let you move them in even more directions — increasing the ergonomic advantage of the mounts even further — but even basic models should confer significant advantages relative to using the monitors with the piece of plastic that was originally provided. There's one other cool thing that monitor mounts can do. Many monitor mount users haven't thought about this (or taken advantage of it!) but you can even rotate them ninety degrees and opt to use one monitor — or your only one — in document (portrait) view. You'll just need to "tell" your display manager that by choosing the right setting in your operating system's display manager — usually called 'orientation'.

The Advantage of Using Multiple Monitors

Notice that I said 'monitors' — in the plural. That's because I recommend that you consider adding at least a second if you currently only have one. More is not necessarily merrier and there are even a few contrarians that prefer one over many. Their line of contention is usually that limiting pixel real estate to one screen is better for focus and they say that it helps them avoid the tendency to multitask that multimonitor computing sometimes arouses simply because there's more than enough screen real estate to do so.

While I'm certainly as guilty as many of being highly distractable when working — in fact probably more so — I disagree with their line of reasoning. Personally if you're going to be engaging in most common freelance occupations — writing, graphic designing, audio engineering, and programming all spring readily to mind — then you'll be hard pressed to find an instance in which having a second screen *isn't* highly beneficial to your productivity (and studies confirm that the productivity gains are real rather than imagined). To round off the ergonomic picture, don't forget to go for a *comfortable* as well as an ergonomic desk and chair and ensure pleasant lighting in your home office. Other nice gadgets to fit out in your workstation are ergonomic mice and keyboards and padding of various sorts — including edge protectors — which is designed to decrease the wear and tear on your elbows. These are particularly useful if you're prone to an arthritic condition that renders these joints more likely to become painful and inflamed by the unconscious grazing that many of us do while moving back and forth to a keyboard.

Peripherals: Mechanical Keyboards

On the keyboard front (and only because this is a technical book!) mechanical keyboards have grown increasingly popular in recent years. Mechanical keyboards are interesting insofar as they represent an unusual process of reversal in technology. Those that remember IBM Model Ms — now collector items — know that most keyboards used to be made with mechanical mechanisms under each keycap such as buckling springs. When computing accelerated greatly in popularity, however, keyboard manufacturers turned to cheap rubber dome mechanisms instead. If you lift up the keycaps on your average keyboard (a simple plastic knife should be all that is needed to apply the required leverage — but do this at your own risk) you may be aghast to notice that when you press a key you are simply pushing down on a piece of rubber membrane.

Mechanical keyboards turn this lamentable state of affairs and this sad and unusual story of technical regression on its head and, for a small sum of money, bring afficionados back to the good old days when manufacturers cared more about the tactile experience of typing than the unit cost. In a mechanical keyboard, each keycap is attached to a mechanical switch. But because every niche within technology has to have enough options to turn into a rabbit hole for those that like tunneling down them (and those people include me), there are a plurality of switch types available to choose between rather than just one. Thus one finds the clicky tactile MX Cherry Blue switches and the more vanilla MX Browns which are ideally weighted — say some, but not others — for everyday typing. There are several switch manufacturers besides Cherry and many different types of switches beyond the two that I mentioned. If you are interested in trying a few out without buying a whole chest-full of keyboards, then you can buy a simple testing board on Amazon or eBay. Although some would say that typing on mechanical keyboards is vastly superior to doing so their rubber dome based cousins which now thoroughly dominate the market, ergonomic keyboards, rather than mechanical ones, are likely to confer larger ergonomic gains. There is a very small number of keyboards which are both driven by mechanical switches *and* which are built in a special layout designed for ergonomics. Enough time searching and reading reviews can usually yield the right product for you.

Non-QWERTY Keyboard Layouts

Finally — and while we're on the topic of typing — it's worth briefly mentioning that there are a couple of keyboard layouts for typing in the English language other than QWERTY which is the standard keyboard layout that you probably use virtually every day.

Dvorak and Colemak are two of the best known non-standard variants and some argue that typing in them is both faster and more ergonomic than it is when doing so with QWERTY. Relearning a keyboard isn't a small endeavor, however. Nor is it one that should be undertaken without first researching whether learning one of these alternative layouts is likely to be useful. There is one additional significant setback to be aware of: the vast majority of English keyboards in the world are set up to type in the QWERTY layout. Ever stroll into a hotel business center and find that the keyboard layout was set up in Dvorak? Nor have I. While most operating systems allow one to easily add different keyboard layouts, or change between them, this feature is not always accessible to end users without administrator permissions. For the sake of not being an extreme contrarian, it is therefore sometimes simply easier to swim with the moving tide of humanity's assumed group preference. I promise to interject the same warning when I finally get around to endorsing Linux as an operating system for the desktop.

Acoustic Devices

While open office layouts seem to be finally winning a well-deserved place in the annals of ill-conceived workplace layouts that are actually horrible for human productivity (and happiness), working from the "comfort" of a home office may not be quite the distraction-free experience that many planning to transition to it envision.

If you've been working from home during recent months, you may already have become well-acquainted with this fact. If you haven't yet happened upon this discovery, then working for a few days at home might be enough for you to discover that garbage men collecting rubbish can seem *very* loud while one is trying to polish off a white paper or work on the last edits for a video. Similarly, the sounds of cats *meowing* seems to coincide with your peak periods of creative focus. Need I go on?

As a noise-sensitive writer dealing with such auditory affronts, and others, has become something of a way of life for me.

If the vicissitudes of life mean that you have been forced to lead an existence as a humble renter rather than homeowner, then you might find that doing things like installing elaborate soundproofing solutions are beyond the limits of what your tenancy agreement allows. Triple-glaze windows sound great, don't they? But, as a humble renter — at the bottom rung of the modern system of feudalism, if you will — some alterations may not be possible until you own your own place (if that day arises –
but I digress). At this stage of the battle, and until you can build a soundproof shell for yourself to work in, two allies can be instrumental companions in one's battle against distracting noise: a white noise generator and a pair of "noise blocking" headphones.

Let me add a little bit of information on this front.

Why Passive Noise Isolation Trumps ANC For Filtering Voices

When people are looking for headphones for this purpose, those based on Active Noise Cancellation (ANC) are typically what come to mind. Think Bose Quietcomfort and the like.

Unfortunately, understanding how ANC works makes it clear why these are actually suboptimal tools for the job. ANC headphones leverage the power of a small embedded microphone which listen to the noises coming from the outside world and then play an opposing frequency to mask them. This is, in effect, selective sound masking which — incidentally — is generally greatly preferable to using white noise for the same purpose (white noise consists of an equal selection of different frequencies played at the same volume. It's an effective tool for sound masking but, played at volume, can be quite grating).

If you've ever used ANC headphones while on a long haul airplane flight and found that the headphones did a stellar job at completely taking away the sound of the aircraft's jet engines then now you understand why this is: the engines emit a fairly predictable pitch. So so long as the thrust used by the pilots remains relatively constant all the headphones had to do was play an opposing frequently in order to mute out the sound (the modulation and frequency-opposing process can happen quickly enough that changes in the composition of sound to be masked can be easily dealt with). But human voices, which are what people commonly want ANC headphones for, needless to say, do not tend to remain at a steady pitch like a jet engine. Instead they modulate continuously in frequency: to simply emit words, to frame questions with the use of unpredictable intonation, or simply to express incredulity at the noisiness of one's work surroundings.

For that reason, headphones which operate by *passively* blocking out sound are a much better choice in this instance. Have you ever pressed your fingers into your ears and found that the world is a much quieter environment as a result? If so, then you are familiar with how passive sound isolation works (a small amount of of hearing actually takes place via bone conduction; but not a significant enough amount to be of relevance for this purpose).

Passive isolation headphones are the type that you press into your ears and the sound comes from the buds. You may just know these as 'headphones' but you probably know the type I'm referring to. In Ear Monitors (IEMs) are simply souped-up variants of this product class — the type which can be found on most high street audio and cellphone stores. They're so called because musicians performing on stage clearly do not want to be deafened by the sound of their own performance. Passive sound isolation is required. But they also need to hear themselves perform: to listen to what, in sound engineering, is commonly called a monitor feed. The amount of passive sound isolation that IEMs offer is commonly equivalent to that of ear plugs (there's a scale for this called the Noise Reduction Ratio, denoted NRR). Etymotic, which started out as a specialist audiology supplier, has carved out a well-deserved reputation for making the IEMs with just about the best isolation in the business. And, indeed, used properly, they offer about the same level as earplugs. If, like me, you find it hard to work when you can't drown out the sound of voices in the background, then I highly recommend that you invest in a pair. You can play white noise through them and mask virtually anything happening in the outside world.

You may recall that we touched upon sound masking just now when discussing IEMs. White noise machines are devices which are designed to simply emit white noise — although most, these days, offer pink and brown noise as well and many can play different background tracks designed for sound masking purposes (such as the sound of rain falling). If you're also in the sound-sensitive bracket then one of these might be useful for your home office too. Although you could achieve almost the same effect by simply playing white noise through any speaker having a dedicated hardware device for this purpose simplifies things. Finally, a word of warning. If you're *really really* adverse to noises then you might have a medical condition. Misophonia, hyperaucusis, and Attention Deficit Disorder (ADD) are all potential causes. Getting it checked out by a doctor is well-advised.

The Computer Itself

So: what kind of *computer* do I recommend that you buy?

That's really beyond the scope of this tech primer and depends on too many factors most of which are individual to the potential user.

I run a Linux-based desktop that uses surprisingly light hardware by today's standards — although I have filled it up with plenty of RAM and have added a few extra SSDs for storing backups (one of those is an onsite backup, which we will cover later). I mention this as one of the few plugs for Linux that I will indulge myself in: because if you're looking for an operating system that's incredibly forgiving to old hardware then a lightweight Linux distribution is your best choice bar none. But assuming you're not trying to breathe life into an old machine, the best computer for you really depends on your individual needs and preferences. And as this text is written for both, say, freelance writers (minimal resource usage) and freelance video editors (high resource usage) making one set of recommendations would both not be prudent and date this text.

However, some generalizations can nevertheless be made and the hardware components which are common to all computers can certainly be explained.

One of those generalizations is that it's prudent to err on the side of going for a greater specification than you think you'll need than winding up with an underpowered device (and this holds especially true for laptop computers which cannot be modified anywhere near as easily as desktops can be). And if you're going to be working with a machine for the majority of your waking hours then I would suggest that your computer is a *very* obvious place in which to invest whatever financial resources you might have to dedicate towards your working capital.

And don't forget to future-proof. Your video rendering rig might be high end by today's standards, but it's worth asking yourself whether it is going to be able to handle the editing workloads that your clients might require in a year or two's time. If you like the idea of multiple monitors, for instance, then you might, at some point, want to add a second graphics card in order to drive the number of displays you require. Perhaps, for instance, you're a day trader that wants to build an outlandish eight monitor array (and in reality day traders are one of the few occupations that wouldn't think of an eight monitor setup as outlandish!) Does the motherboard of what you are thinking of buying have two PCI Express 16 slots to allow for expansion or only one? Will the power supply unit (PSU) support the cumulative demands of the graphics cards you want to plug into the machine? And if you need the (desktop version) of the Microsoft Office suite in order to stay productive is this included in the license and preinstalled with the computer? Ask yourself questions and invest appropriately in what's likely to yield the best ROI for your freelance business over time.

Basic Computer Hardware Explained

But just so that you know what you're buying, even in very rough terms, let me explain what the various hardware components of a computer do.

That way, when it comes time to make your big purchase, you can piece together what the various resources are there to make happen.

CPU: The CPU, commonly referred to as the 'processor' is the central processing unit of the computer. You can think of it as the computer's "brain". The type of CPU you choose will have a great effect upon how the computer performs and particularly its ability to perform multiple tasks at once. If you're involved in rendering video, sound, or complex photography projects for instance then you probably already have an idea of what CPU you want — or at least the manufacturer and generation.

RAM: Random Access Memory is a type of volatile storage that the computer uses to store data in that is not going to be required after reboot and which is not, therefore, permanently written to a disk (the latter type of storage, like the data stored on an SSD disk, is known as persistent storage and survives reboots — and clearly this is the type of storage that an operating system needs to live on.) As a volatile form of memory, RAM can be read or changed in any order. Data stored on RAM can be read or written in almost the same time irrespective of where, physically, it is stored on the RAM stick.

The amount of RAM you'll need in a computer depends, really, on how many resources (services and processes) you typically use at any one time. Are you a freelance writer that typically works on a Word (or LibreOffice) document with a couple of browser tabs open for reference? If so, the amount of RAM you require will be very modest and likely just about anything on today's market is going to be adequate for your needs. Or are you, by way of comparison, a freelance video editor that is constantly rendering high definition (HD) video projects for clients, something several at a time? In that case, your RAM requirement will be a lot higher than that of the freelance writer. One final detail while we're talking about typical RAM consumption levels. It's worth knowing that the Google

Chrome browser, in particular, consumes a lot of RAM: that's because (at least at the time of writing) each tab creates a separate computing process — and these are what add up to create a RAM overhead. If you often use 50 or 60 Chrome tabs spread across three screens — *and* you often virtualize another operating system while you do so (we'll cover virtualization in the chapter on web hosting) — then even 20GB of RAM might be insufficient as a RAM allocation for your needs.

The maximum amount of RAM which your computer can work with is determined, in turn, by your motherboard — and when one resource is capped by another in computing it tends to be referred to as a 'bottleneck' for obvious reasons (in this case, the motherboard might be a bottleneck to the amount of RAM that you can run; and that, in turn might bottleneck what you can do with the computer). Clearly, if you're planning on buying a computer but are already thinking in terms of future upgrades, then you'll want to make sure that the components you start with won't stand in the way of one another when it becomes time to do bigger things with your hardware. If you're running a desktop solution then the motherboard is typically the last component that you think about upgrading and the most likely component to be that final bottleneck in the chain: so many components are attached to it that it can be quite a hassle to replace or upgrade it and even many enthusiasts, at this point, prefer to start a new build afresh rather than disassemble and reassemble components and wires. All the more so for laptops. Laptop motherboards cannot generally be upgraded at all — at least not without entailing an extraordinary degree of difficulty.

But that's thinking down the line. If right now all you need is a bit more RAM then fortunately, so long as you stay below your motherboard's capacity, the job of upgrading it is relatively easy. You *can* generally add RAM to both laptops and desktops by either swapping out a smaller capacity RAM stick for a larger one or by adding more RAM to a spare bay if one exists (as mentioned, up to the limit of the motherboard; and if you don't what that limit is you can usually easily retrieve the specifications online — and that goes for all mainstream hardware components). In the broad scheme of computer upgrades, upgrading RAM is both relatively easy and inexpensive.

Graphics Card / GPU: The Graphical Processing Unit (GPU) is the part of the computer that is responsible for driving the creation of physical images to represent computing processes. In other words, it allows users to hook monitors up to computers in order to do things like manipulate computing processes with Graphical User Interfaces (GUIs) — as distinct from servers which we'll come back to when we look at setting up cloud infrastructure later. This feed of images is contained within a frame buffer and outputted onto some physical display device such as — again — a monitor, although it could equally be the built-in display on a laptop. All desktops and laptops have an integrated graphics card — because otherwise viewing their processes on a display wouldn't be possible at all. This integrated graphics card is built into the CPU and draws a small amount of memory from it allow it to operate. In other words, it doesn't have a discrete memory supply. Users that want higher performance, however, typically opt for a dedicated GPU — and when we're talking about 'graphics cards' then this is what we are, in fact, referring to. These GPUs are added to the motherboard by (physically) pushing them into an open slot and higher end motherboards can support more than one (for instance, dual GPU setups). Dedicated GPUs, by contrast with the integrated ones built into CPUs, have their own memory and receive a dedicated power supply from the power supply unit (PSU) in the computer. Speaking of bottlenecks, PSUs are commonly bottlenecks for GPU upgrades: before choosing one for your computer, you'll need to know what wattage (W) the manufacturer recommends that it receives — and select a PSU that can both accommodate that as well as the other draws required by various components of your system. If you're buying a desktop, you'll have to decide whether you want a dedicated GPU at all. If you're buying a laptop then you will more typically simply use whatever is provided to drive the display.

Storage devices: You might remember the days when files and folders were written onto thin square objects called 'floppy disks' which were shoved into post box-like slots on the front of computers in order to read and write data. Of course these days, if we're still using small transportable storage media at all that is, we're more likely to be attaching a USB drive to a USB slot. However, those, of course, are not the only storage volumes that a computer will typically use during operation. Inside the computer, hidden from view, there are a number of permanently attached drives that store the operating system and all the data that is held on a computer. Remember the all-important motherboard that determined how much RAM we could add to a computer and which is, in essence, the central piece of hardware in a computer? The same goes for storage devices: we can only attach as many drives as our motherboard physically has slots for (typically nowadays these are SATA ports). Unlike USB ports, SATA port splitting isn't a 'thing' — so if you're looking to do something unusual like attach 6 drives to your computer, a low-end motherboard might prove to be — again — a bottleneck. If you're buying a desktop PC off the shelf — or a laptop — then it's very unlikely that the type of motherboard within the build is going to be explicitly stated.

Instead, you'll need to pay careful attention to the technical specifications, which might mention how far each hardware component, such as RAM, can be expanded (e.g. "16GB RAM. Supported: up to 64GB").

Regardless of whether it's within a desktop, a laptop, or a server, disk storage tends to be measured these days in either gigabytes (GB) or terabytes (TB). And the higher the number the more information the drive can store (drives are sometimes still called 'disks' even though clearly most internal storage media these days, namely SSDs, have no mechanized spinning disk component). Speaking of units of measurement for disk capacity and storage: there are greater units than terabytes. Petabytes (PB; 1000 TB), Exabytes (EB, roughly 1,00 PB), and even loftier storage volumes exist too. It's just that — at the point in time when this text is being written — it's rare to find drives that large within reasonable budgets . And again, when we're talking about expansion capacities and how far hardware can be pushed, the motherboard is typically the ultimate constraint.

The Evolving Forms of Storage

The type of storage in widespread use slowly but constantly evolves — as our earlier reference to the now deprecated floppy disks underscored. Hard drives (hard disk drives / HDDs) have, for most intents and purposes, bit the dust (exception: backup storage; rationale: HDDs are still quite a bit cheaper). Instead, solid state drives (SSDs) have offered a quieter replacement without physical moving parts — and they also offer vastly superior read/write speeds.

At the time of writing, NVMe is emerging as the latest and greatest breed of storage media for both desktop and server usage. It is available in a number of common form factors — which means that it is physically compatible with a lot of modern hardware if they have the right connection ports. NVMe, which is a type of SSD, offers superior sustained read/write speeds compared to conventional SSDs (which, in turn as we saw, offer superior read/write speeds, and thus a faster computing experience, compared to the hard drives of yonder). NVMe is the next logical evolution in the market and so — as always happens — can be expected to gradually replace current SSDs, although the process typically takes many years and is followed by a protracted period of dual support. Undoubtedly, however, HDDs will ultimately become totally obsolete — much as floppy disks are in mainstream computing. If you are old enough to still be well-acquainted with hard drives, or that scratchy sound they sometimes make when on the verge of failing, then you will, some day soon, become a historical curiosity — just as your parents who can tell tales of the travails of backing up the year's accounting records onto a slew of floppy disks are now.

Other Hardware Components

The above list is not intended to be an exhaustive run-through of the various hardware components and peripherals which might comprise your typical computer.

For instance, your average computer needs to be kept cool with a number of fans. Typically cases (the box within which PC components live) include at least three fans. If you're installing a dedicated GPU then it has its own cooling mechanism too. The purpose of these fans is — unsurprisingly, and as the name suggests — to keep the components cool. The main drawback of fans is that they make noise — and, as you might remember from earlier in this chapter, I disclosed that I am adverse to distracting noises. If, again, you share in my acoustic predicament, then you should look specifically for fans that are rated to emit lower amounts of noise, although these usually will come at a higher price tag than their noisier counterparts. Better yet, you could opt to cool your PC with a water cooling system.

Additionally, you're probably going to need a couple more cards which will attach to the motherboard — again, depending upon what you want to do with your computer.

For instance, unless you're going to be freelancing on-site for an energy manufacturer in one of those ultra-secure air-gapped networks I mentioned earlier (and I'm going to go out on a limb and guess that you are not!), you're almost certainly going to want to have a network card in your PC. If you're buying a laptop then you have no need to worry: these are already built in. If you're buying a desktop and intend connecting with WiFi to your home internet, then it almost goes without saying that you should opt for a network card that has WiFi receivers. These support slightly different WiFi standards. See what your router transmits at and pick an appropriate card. They are relatively inexpensive.

Motherboards have integrated sound cards — as they do graphics cards. But unlike the graphics cards that are built into their circuitry, these are almost always sufficient for the needs of basic users. If, however, you want something more advanced — say, an XLR port to plug instruments into and receive digital, rather than analog, inputs — then you will probably want to opt instead for a dedicated sound card.

Microphones, Headsets, and Webcams: The Videoconferencing Arsenal

Finally, as a freelancer coming of age in this day and age, you are almost certain to be spending a disconcerting amount of time asserting the strength of your "value proposition" on Zoom meetings with participants around the world (I try my hardest not to lapse into corporate jargon, but sometimes do so intentionally just to delight a little in its ridiculousness).

Sadly, not having hard a haircut for months no longer seems to cut it as a good enough excuse for evading these virtual meetings. So, in addition to having to grovel with complete strangers to hire you for a temporary freelancing opp, you will also be expected to suffer the additional indignity of having to do so while beaming a video feed of your visage to complete strangers observing you from behind their computers on the other side of the globe (potentially). Videoconferencing is thus insipidly depriving freelancers of the right to work in their pajamas and so the exploding popularity of platforms such as Zoom is one change which should be met with caution as well as joy.

In order to hold a videoconference you are also clearly going to need a microphone to speak into and some kind of audio device to play back the sound from the other end — as well as that webcam we reluctantly concluded is required. Again, the laptop:desktop dichotomy looms large here. Laptops typically have all of these things built into them: the webcam is usually positioned atop the built-in display, there's a small microphone somewhere you can't see (it usually loops like a tiny pin-hole), as well as speakers which could be positioned toward the underside of the computer.

If you're going to buy a desktop then (unless you've opted for a monitor that has one built in) you'll need to buy an external webcam that connects over USB. You'll want to buy a microphone too — or else a headset which combines both over-ear headphones *and* a microphone in one device. If, like me, you lean towards taking steps to protect your privacy, then you'll also want to find a software solution for disabling the built-in microphone on your laptop (this is one advantage of desktops). It may sound like something from a movie, but hackers remotely activating your peripherals — via spyware programs or some other illicit means — is a credible threat even if it's a relatively remote one. Think people listening in to your audio feed. Not cool.

Beyond making sure that you *have* one of both a microphone and a webcam you might be wondering how should you select *which* model from the ever-bulging marketplace from which you can choose?

For webcams, the most important distinction (and this goes for laptops' built-in webcams too) is the resolution which it can drive.

High definition (HD) video is *de rigeur* in today's world, but it commonly comes in two standards one better than the other: 720P (which consists of a 1280x720 pixel video feed) and 1080P (which consists of a 1920 x1080 pixel video feed). I recommend shelling out the premium for a webcam that can drive a video feed at the latter (1080P), higher resolution. Displaying a 'full HD' video feed on your next Zoom meeting with a prospective client will further the professional impression you seek, so earnestly, to give off. And offering up a grainy low quality video feed from your smartphone as you pilot your bicycle through a nature trail will likely do the opposite (I speak from personal experience being on the receiving end of this kind of call). Likewise, one should ideally take pains to invest in a good quality headset or microphone — as the quality of these, needless to say, will determine the audio quality which the other side receives. All the above applies even if your computer (say, your laptop) has built-in peripherals. There's nothing stopping you from plugging in a better webcam, for instance, and improving upon the quality which the integrated camera your laptop shipped with can deliver.

One final note about privacy.

Nothing creeps me out more than the thought of somebody spying on me through my webcam: observing a video feed of me from some shady den of cybercrooks while I go about my daily day's work. *Yes*, webcams generally contain helpful little LED lights which illuminate when active to warn the user that they are in use and capturing video. And *yes* a basic firewall and adhering to simple internet security best practices (like *not* clicking on suspicious requests for webcam access) should be all that is required to obviate this threat. But can you ever feel 100% comfortable placing your face in these software-based protections? Because most of us would find the idea of somebody watching us from our webcam feed so disconcerting, there is also a feeling that one cannot be cautious enough. For that reason many opt for webcam models which contain a physical piece of plastic that pulls over the aperture to prevent the webcam from capturing video. If your webcam doesn't have one, one can usually be bought: just search for the webcam's model and privacy filter. Failing that, cut out a few strips of black insulation tape and place over the camera's opening when not in use. Or, if you're using an external (USB) webcam, you can go one step further and physically disconnect the peripheral when it isn't in use. If you have a laptop, you can buy stickers which are intended to overlay upon the webcam and similarly prevent the video feed through physical means by creating a blockage over the camera. Some laptops even have them built in. In other words, whether you use a desktop or laptop and no matter what type of webcam you own there are usually options. These are prudent practices for anybody concerned about the dangers of unauthorized access to one's peripherals devices.

Power Supply Units (PSUs)

We mentioned the PSU when we were talking, above, about selecting dedicated graphics cards (GPUs). The Power Supply Unit (PSU), commonly just called the 'power supply,' supplies power to all the components of a desktop computer. These convert the Alternating Current (AC) power from the outlet into Direct Current (DC) and then feed that, via cabling, to the various components in a computer. In laptops, the PSU is encased within the "charger" that fulfills the same function. Unless you're upgrading the components of your desktop then this — or fans, which we will skip entirely — are not things that you will need to worry about.

Operating Systems

In order for you to be able to interface with the components in your computer, those which we mentioned above, you are going to need an operating system (OS). Up to this point, we've been talking about the basic *hardware* components that are required to make a computer do useful things. But that's only one type of 'ware' which we are likely to encounter. There's also *firmware* — programs like the Basic Input/Output System (BIOS) that are hard-coded into a computing device and which cannot be easily modified by the user. These need to exist so that — in the case of BIOS — a state can't easily be reached when the computer is so badly damaged that it can't even start up (assuming, that is, that its hardware components are functional). The BIOS, or UEFI (similar but more modern) is typically installed on a non-volatile chunk of Read Only Memory (ROM) which is installed directly onto the motherboard. This ensures that even in a situation whereby the computer's main storage is corrupted beyond repair the user will be able to purchase a new drive and hopefully continue to be able to use the computer. When we talk about backups, we'll get to ways to hedge against the constant threat of disk failure — but the most important thing to know for now is that the average expected service time of SSDs is believed to be around 10 years. Finally, at the top of the 'stack' there is software: the programs required to actually do things with the underlying hardware on a computer. And the operating system is the second-to-top layer in that stack: the basic set of software, including things as simple as a graphics server, upon which other software — such as word processors — are installed.

If you're using a Linux distribution then you don't require that your computer ships with an operating system preinstalled at all: you can easily install one yourself simply by downloading an installation file from the internet, loading it onto a live USB, and following some system prompts. However, for most users, the choice is going to be between whether to purchase a conventional Windows computer, commonly referred to as a PC, or whether to opt for a tool by Apple. Apple desktop and laptop devices run an operating system called MacOS (iOS is for mobile peripherals, namely iPads and iPhones). Linux and Mac are actually relatively closely related. Windows is not. The choice of which operating system you're going to go with again depends mostly upon personal factors and what software you are planning on using with your computer.

Building A Computer

If you get in the habit of talking with technologists, then you will inevitably cross paths with a strange breed of people who build their own computers. You may be wondering whether you, too, should build your own PC — or should you, instead, simply rely upon a machine that HP has decided is good enough for your needs and put into a product catalogue with a predetermined set of components.

Building your own PC naturally allows you to opt for exactly the set of components that you require. On the flip side, it takes some expertise in order to put one together. For most users a premanufactured PC is going to be the obvious choice. But for those that want to dive deep in to learning how all the various hardware components work together the self-directed building approach might be the preferred methodology.

Highly Recommended: Uninterruptible Power Supplies (UPSs)

There's one final piece of gear in my office that I actually recommend that every home office worker pick up. And no, this isn't an affiliate marketing play. That's an Uninterruptible Power Supply (UPS). UPSs are basically small transformer batteries that sit between the outlet and your electronics (that's why they're so heavy). You plug your computer into the back and in the event that the power goes out it will continue to run off it for some minutes. (The moment a power outage is detected the supply instantaneously switches over to the battery.) Cool, no? If you're using a laptop, you can basically say that you are already availing yourself of *some* of the advantages that a UPS brings (although I use the word 'some' advisedly;

UPSs also provide passive surge protection). They come in different capacities and the volt-ampere (VA) and Watts (W) figures are what you'll be wanting to pay attention to. You'll want to make sure that the total wattage which your UPS can supply is ideally greater than the combined draw of all your computer's components plus whatever else you're planning on plugging into it.

There are a few cool advantages that having a UPS in your home office configuration confers. For one, you can plug your router into the UPS (just don't plug in your printer — there's a reason why!). This will mean that — in the event that power goes out — the router will stay online for as long as the UPS can power it and you won't lose your home internet even when the mains power goes down along with your fridge and just about every other appliance at home. If you just have the router on the UPS this should actually be quite a long time as routers are low draw devices. You should also, ideally, run the ethernet connection to your computer through the UPS. If you're connected by ethernet, and you don't, a surge can travel directly through the network cabling into your computer, independently of the power supply. Which might mean bidding a sad and unexpected goodbye to all those delightful (and costly) components we looked at in the previous section of this chapter.

There's another advantage to making sure that *your* freelancing home office setup runs rings around that guy in his pajamas operating out of bed who we imagined our office-working friend making a mental caricature out of earlier. You can plug a desk light into the UPS! If you have all of these components plugged into your UPS at the same time — computer, desk light, and router — then you should be able to keep working through a power outage, at least temporarily, with virtually no discomfort. You just might need a couple of cables to make the magic work (the connection into the UPS is usually C14 and C14 to whatever plug adapters exist in your country can typically be procured for a dollar or two; if you can't find them locally you will almost be certainly able to do so online). As an added bonus, the UPS provides some passive surge protection, helping to protect and extend the useful service time of your electronics by both ensuring a more consistent power supply and preventing hard shutdowns due to loss of power. You'll also look cool too. Unperturbed by lightning, hail, or power surges you can be the iconoclastic image of freelancing resilience continuing to pound away at the keyboard on your desk (almost) no matter what life throws your way.

At the freelance level of scale, there's not much more than that to be known about selecting a good internet connection and equipping yourself with the computer hardware needed to get the job done. And to get it done well well. So let's call it a wrap on chapter one.

In summary:

- An ISP delivers internet connectivity to your home/workplace
- At a very bare minimum, look into what speed is promised and exactly what verbiage underlies that guarantee. As I hinted, there may, in fact, be none at all.
- If you need a guaranteed fast upload speed, or a more robust connection guarantee, then consider business-grade internet. It tends to cost more but, depending on your use, it might be worth it if you can't find a residential package that meets your requirements.
- Don't neglect ergonomics when deciding whether to use a desktop or laptop — and how to set up your home office.
- I highly recommend VESA monitor mounts and working with at least two monitors.

- An uninterruptible power supply (UPS) is a cool thing to have on hand too: you'll be able to wow your friends if they come round to visit right when there's a power cut — but you, the tireless freelancer, are able to carry on working regardless.

2. CREATING A WEB PRESENCE

Setting up the infrastructure to house your forthcoming online empire

So let's do a quick "technology scan" to recap on where we've got to so far.

We've thrown sound reason out the window and embarked upon the modern day gold rush: to make a living from the comfort of our home as a full-time freelancer. But because we're going to be geeking out on the technology front we've decided to equip ourselves with an executive-grade home office and resist the temptation to work from bed.

We've also decided — well, you've decided by picking this book up — that we're going to get our basic technology systems in place *before* it's too late and they become a bottleneck to our productivity. And trust me, this is always recommendable — because no matter what technology you have at your disposal you will find that it tends to have a habit of breaking down at the worst possible moment just as your deadlines are accumulating. This concept appears to hold as true for freelancers as it does for the general public.

We've looked at what factors you'll likely want to consider when deciding upon what byte-dealer to go with (in normal person language that's called an ISP — and I'll have to admit that I just made that term up). We've briefly touched upon why ergonomics are important — namely because you'll be slogging at that laptop like a mule day after day, week after week, slowly ratcheting up line items on those invoices sustaining your existence. And we've even tricked out our home office with some neat power backup systems just because we're going the whole nine yards with this technology stuff.

We're off to a good start — but we have nothing to show for ourselves online yet.

Now, we just need to demonstrate to the exterior world how awesome we are so that we can find people who are willing to pay us currency for our awesomeness (just not in exposure, thank you very much).

It's time for: an online presence.

How a Website Gets On The Internet

When people ask about what's entailed in getting a functional portfolio website onto the internet they tend to do so as if describing a mythological process in which a fully functional website — replete with fancy embedded scripts, stylish graphics, and attention-grabbing widgets — should be expected to magically descend from some upper echelons of the cybersphere.

It's *possible* to use an all-in-one style builder which will take care of all the components that I'm about to describe here. The process might even feel somewhat mythological — even along the lines described. However let me be transparent and state that I am unashamedly against such tools. If freelancing is going to be the centerpoint of your income, then I think it makes a lot of sense to learn how to build real things on the internet — rather than handing over the keys to your online world to some What You See Is What You Get (WYSIWYG) editor that will do everything for you in a jiffy. There's a reason why these all-in-one editors continue to enjoy mass market appeal: things like Drupal websites are certainly harder to put together than template-based pages which you can automagically pull together in five minutes with the help of an AI assistant. But solutions that are just a little bit less "set it and forget it" also stand a much better chance at withstanding the process of scale for a much longer period. (And this isn't an argument against low-code or codeless either: I just think that more mature tools, which let you control the components underlying a website, should be favored above click and point designers which do everything but often leave you in full control of nothing).

Part of what I'm trying to explain here is how everything fits together and works. And trust me, over the long term — particularly if you're planning to scale — many people, including possibly you, will be much happier not having all their online assets locked into any one vendor, no matter how appealing or simplistic their offer might have seemed when you were just getting going with setting up an online shop. This is called vendor lock-in and we'll come back to the concept later when we're looking at why it makes sense to keep backup copies of even the data you host on the cloud — the data which you probably assume is being assiduously backed up by somebody other than you (not a safe bet).

In reality, there are a number of discrete components which go into making a website "come online" on the internet. Fitting them together does not, unfortunately, resemble the mythical process I outlined earlier. It's helpful to know these only insofar as that information is directly relevant to the process of getting a website 'up there'. Even if some of the all-in-one DIY builder tools I mentioned (and which, I realize, still might sound more appealing) obfuscate all these details from you in the name of user-friendliness and easy UI. Let's take a look at them, starting with the most basic facet of a website: its URL.

What's A 'Domain Name' Really?

The first thing that one needs in order to operate a website is a domain name.

When you first heard about computers you might have heard these referred to as Uniform Resource Locators (URLs). To get technical on just this one detail: they are not exactly the same thing; a URL is just a complete web address and a domain is the x.tld identified used to specify the online home of your website.

Here's, in brief, how acquiring and leasing a domain works.

Each Top Level Domain (the thing after your website — '.com', '.co.uk', '.ie' - etc) is really one big register. A massive one, in fact. And you, a prospective website owner, can rent an alphanumeric entry in that register, for a specified time period. This record will then be propagated into a worldwide network called the Domain Name System (DNS). You will then create records to be sent to this system which will tell those placing queries to it (internet browsers) which public IP addresses to direct queries for that domain name, or parts of it, to. For the end user, the person browsing the internet who you hope might be interested in using your freelance services, this means that they will simply have to type in yourdomain.com to a browser to get to your website — instead of plucking away at a numeric keypad to input an awkward series of numbers such as 172.212.13.123 (which, in this instance, might represent the public IP address of the server you are hosted on). You may never *need* to know or remember this. But it might be helpful to know a little later.

So who are the people that will sell you a line in the '.com' register for a specific time period, you may be wondering?

These would be domain registrars — and there are a lot of them, some of which have become relatively famous (as far as tech companies involved in hosting goes engaging in prime time advertising probably automatically qualifies). Most hosting companies these days are also domain registrars: they try to encourage you to sign up for their hosting packages by offering a "free" domain — and then, unless you want to go through the process of transferring the domain out, you are stuck with them. But there is almost never anything stopping you from hosting and managing a domain name with separate companies (so long as your nameservers are pointed correctly — or they are pointed to your Cloudflare nameservers, and then those DNS records are correctly configured.)

Now, not every registrar deals with every top level domain (TLD) in existence. And new TLDs are constantly coming onto the hosting market in an intricate approval process that you don't need to know about but which occasionally makes the news whenever a particularly outlandish new TLD is proposed. So, if you want something slightly more exotic — such as a .agency, for instance, which is rising in popularity among marketing agencies these days— then your options might be more limited. Additionally, some registrars might enforce specific registration criteria for buying a domain with a certain TLD — such as insisting that the company be a non-profit or have a registered business address in the country if it is a geography-specific TLD such as '.co.uk'. Most probably, however, you will look to purchase a '.com'. You may have SEO reasons for wanting to favor the most vanilla option out there — and the .com vs. everything else debate is one that I am not qualified to even begin to address (the digital side of marketing has never particularly interested me but there are a plethora of experts who have wisdom to bestow on this question and many more). If you are indeed, as I surmise, interested in hosting your website as a .com then you will have no shortage of options to choose from. Go with whichever registrar or package looks best to you.

Finding An Online Home For Your Website

As I hope the above made clear, buying a domain name is not the start and end of setting up a website but rather only the first step in the journey towards putting it online.

Actually, as we saw, buying a domain name simply buys you the *ability* to direct people towards an alphanumeric internet address which you can *then* configure to automatically forward to a public IP address by DNS! And when you stop to think about it for a moment, the sole intent of all this digital trickery which we call renting domain names is to save your loyal customers — and yourself — the mental aggravation of having to remember a long list of numbers when they want to go about their daily internet browsing activity. *"Is Google.com at 170.08.48 or 170.08.32 today"* — is a conversation that you, like I, have probably never overheard when buying milk at the local grocery store.

Buying a domain name doesn't actually get a website "on the internet" *per se*. Because in order to have a website you need somewhere to store the information it contains (and by that I mean the files and databases that are going to serve the dynamic content your visitors will be expecting to receive whenever they visit it). Besides having the files and folders in place somewhere in the cloud, there needs to be some computer that can serve that content to users that have expressed an interest in viewing it (by typing your site's address into their web browser). This entails — as the name suggests — setting up infrastructure to serve the website from. And in this case the required infrastructure would be a webserver.

To introduce a slight technicality, and to strive for accuracy, I should tell you that you don't actually strictly *need* a third party (like a web hosting company) to succeed in this endeavor of trying to set up a website on your newly acquired domain name.

This isn't the right book to read if you're more interested in the DIY approach than doing things the conventional way — it would likely be far too basic for your needs if you were. But suffice to say that you *can* host your own websites using nothing more sophisticated than a spare laptop running something like Ubuntu's sever edition. To make this work you'd simply need to change the port forwarding settings on your router so that those beyond your home network can send in the requests to see the websites which it serves (and that's only because those providing residential internet connections, the ISPs we mentioned in chapter one, do not typically expect their customers to use their internet connectivity to operate amateur data centers). Oh, and I forgot to mention that you'll need to leave that laptop or computer running 24/7. Unless you want your website to have operating hours. Which would be an interesting eccentricity to attempt to foist on the world. But which probably wouldn't succeed in winning you much business. For these and other reasons (we didn't even consider the cybersecurity aspect) almost everybody these days hosts their sites commercially.

Hosting companies specialize in providing online space for people like you and I to host our websites on. People like you and I who have determined that (sadly) the leaving a laptop on all the time approach isn't the best fit for our needs.

75

Even from a societal standpoint, everybody hosting websites on their own network would be both unwieldy and impracticable. Pooling resources together and entrusting the job to professional hosting companies simply makes a lot more sense. When customers so pool their financial resources together by purchasing their services, hosting companies can afford to employ teams of professional system administrators (commonly called sysadmins) to make sure that the websites hosted on their servers are properly secured by things like Web Application Firewalls / WAFs. This fact alone significantly reduces the chance that a cybercrook will be able to take certain actions, like flooding a site with traffic, that might force sites such as yours off the internet. And they can afford to make sure that the infrastructure they operate to provide hosting services from are professionally managed — by paying those system administrators to look after the network, keep everything well upgraded, and troubleshoot any issues that may arise during routine operation. They can also do fancy things like ensure that they have backup power sources so that those customers can be reasonably well-assured that the servers won't randomly go offline even if the data centers falls victim to a power surge (these are known as uptime guarantees — and you can think of the backup power systems in place at professional data centers as the industrial equivalent of the humble home UPS devices we looked at in chapter one). Professional hosts, especially cloud hosting providers, can also mirror data across difference physical storage locations to create redundancy. Finally, they can also use the money that their customers pay them to hire support people to help customers resolve any issues they have using the service (technical support)— although in practice you will find that many hosting companies outsource tier one support and that the quality of it can be very hit or miss. This, in a nutshell, is why hosting companies exist and why you'll be needing to deal with one (even if the hosting is wrapped up in a comprehensive 'package' and never referred to by name). And they're the people you'll want to get in touch with if you want to find an online home to "store" your website.

You might quickly discover, however, that the hosting packages which they sell, like home internet connections, come in various shapes and sizes. Hosting, after all, is not a homogeneous activity and various companies need it at markedly different levels of scale: Amazon.com has to find somewhere to host all the files, databases, and scripts it uses to power its online global marketplace and so too *you*, a minnow of the hosting world, need to find a home for your crummy portfolio site containing a headshot, a few PDFs, and a 'contact me' form. (Actually, Amazon is so large that it has spun out its own infrastructure into a self-standing product: known as Amazon Web Services but more commonly simply referred to by its acronym of AWS.)

For this reason, hosting companies offer different products for both the titans of this world and the small fish like ourselves.

But for the sake of completion — and because freelancers sometimes turn into agencies and agencies sometimes turn into multinational companies — let's run through the most common options that you might be trying to decide between when looking at your hosting options.

Shared Hosting: The Cheap And (Hopefully) Cheerful Option

The most basic of hosting setups is known as shared hosting.

And if shared hosting were an airline it would be a no frills discount operator that might skimp a little on the pleasantries but usually manages to get your files to its destination (visitors' computers) reasonably close to on time.

With shared hosting you, and a bunch of other customers, are hosted on the same physical server — nestled in some data farm that the hosting company operates, sometimes in the middle of the Nevada desert. In exchange for your subscription fee, you receive a filesystem within the server whereupon you can typically add both a "primary domain" as well as addon domains if you're going to be hosting more than one website on the shared hosting account. You will, in practice, be 'caged' to operating within a subdirectory of a folder within the server and you'll also need to keep all your various websites, files, and folders within that folder. These technical nuances might seem small but as we will see later they do, in fact, they matter.

Sometimes, shared hosts set some limit as to how many websites you can add under one shared hosting plan — although there is a general trend, well in train at the time of writing, towards competing based on 'unlimited' resources (as with cellphone plans, it's worth scrutinizing the fine print of what's being offered nonetheless — it's highly unlikely that you *won't* run into difficulties if you find a way to upload terabytes of data to your shared hosting account.)

The Deficiencies of Shared Hosting

The single filesystem that we discussed earlier certainly makes the job of administering several websites from one cPanel trivially easy. However, it also introduces an important vulnerability. Because your "websites" are all just subdirectories within a directory (think subfolders on your desktop — it's the same concept just on a remote computer) they are susceptible to cross-site contamination due to poor isolation. Caging can prevent this (we'll mention that again later, but it's a good reason to consider upgrading to reseller hosting). Cross-site contamination means that if, for instance, one site is infected with malware then it can simply hop across to the next directory and infect that site too. Think of a virus spreading between directories in your computer and rendering folders nearly useless as it does so. And so on and so forth (scenarios like this are partially why it's very important to take good backups of your online hosting — even if the hosting company clearly does too).

There are other issues too that fall into the broader category of so-called 'bad neighbor' problems. This somewhat colorful name is an apt description for the type of problems that can result from problematic co-tenants on the server your shared hosting account actually lives on. You know what sites you are hosting (presumably!) but not those which other customers are placing on the same server that your data lives on. And, very broadly speaking, if these other websites in your building (by which I mean server) prove to be problematic in some way then this could have a knock-on effect for the performance of your own web properties.

From a resource allocation standpoint there are also some deficiencies to the shared hosting paradigm that it is important to be aware of if you are looking to scale your online business rapidly. The server's resources are being allocated dynamically to those different customers. This means that it's possible that a surge in traffic to a co-tenant on the server will temporarily degrade performance to your sites as your competitor's website takes up things like CPU and RAM on the server. A denial of service (DDoS) cyberattack on your neighbor might also catch your online property in its dragnet by flooding the server with so many requests from a botnet (when targeting a common IP rather than a website hosted on that server IP) that the server is unable to serve any traffic at all. And if *your* online properties begin hogging up too much resources then *you* might find your websites being artificially slowed down (throttled) in order to ensure that the same thing doesn't happen to the people living next door (other users' sites on the same server).

If you're not raking in the visitors, then this is a perfectly fine arrangement and these inherent deficiencies are likely to be manageable even if they're not necessarily ideal. But if you're scaling up traffic wise you're going to be better off with some kind of hosting setup that *does* guarantee you a certain level of stable fixed computing resources.

What *should* you look for in that case?

Servers, like computers, have hardware and software resources that influence their performance (a type of CPU, an amount of RAM, a variant of an operating system — the factors we looked at in chapter one) — although as I mentioned the resource share usually isn't guaranteed in shared hosting configurations. There's one important distinction between servers and desktops, however, that you should be aware of: Servers generally run a distribution of Linux whereas in desktop-land Linux has always attracted only a tiny share of the market (comprised mostly of zealots like me who realize that it makes their day-to-day life needlessly difficult but enjoy, nevertheless, the teaching experience that it provides.) So if you're evaluating a VPS for instance (we'll look at those in turn), you will probably want to be think about whether an Ubuntu server, a Debian server, one running Fedora, or a Windows server will best meet your needs. In shared hosting your line of questioning during the evaluation process can be more rudimentary.

Consider asking:

- Is there a limit to the number of files and folders I can store on this shared hosting account ? (This is known as an inode limit; plans with unlimited storage might add this requirement to prevent egregious abuse.)
- Is there a limit to how much disk space I can use?
- Is there a limit to how many email accounts I can create on the server?

As a shared hosting customer you will be able to make some basic configuration changes to the server by interfacing with a tool hosted by your webhost. Most typically, this will be cPanel (far fewer offer a tool called Plesk). And if you host for any length of time you will become intimately familiar with its functionalities.

However, when I talk about making configuration changes here I'm talking, really, about making a series of tightly defined changes like setting up email addresses and forwarders, editing DNS entries, and editing the files, or databases, on the server.

What I'm *not* talking about is doing administrative level modifications such as installing packages onto the server or managing its basic configuration in any way (like attaching more disk space). This would require root (administrator-level) access and in the latter case you'd need to either upgrade to another plan with your host or use some type of hosting that allows you to dynamically scale resources (such as AWS EC2 - a form of on-demand elastic cloud hosting which we will look at later in this chapter).

Shared hosting environments do not provide such options — and the add-ons that many hosts will try to upsell you on will not really change the picture in any substantive way. As you get further into your journey with technology, the problems that this may cause you might begin to slowly manifest. If you begin running software on the server which requires certain server packages that your host has not provisioned, for instance, then the user limit limitation might start to become a big issue. We'll talk about that when we look at open source and server scripts later on.

Reseller Hosting

Despite the foregoing problems, many freelancers will do just fine with a shared hosting configuration — potentially, in fact, for quite a long time.

But there's another form of relatively cheap and cheerful hosting that in many cases might provide a better fit — especially for freelancers that are operating multiple websites. It is called reseller hosting.

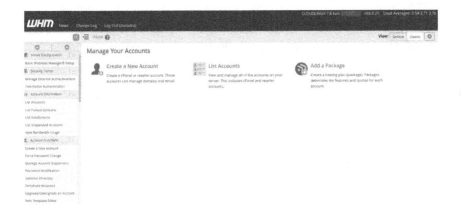

I have previously (and somewhat jocularly) referred to reseller hosting as the web hosting industry's best kept secret. And that's because some assume that it can only be purchased by those reselling web hosting — which is its intended purpose after all. Others simply gloss over it entirely because they figure that as they're not a reseller and have no intention of ever being one they couldn't have use for reseller web hosting. Neither assumption is true.

Reseller hosting certainly *can* be used to set up your very own hosting company — effectively white-labeling another host's access to infrastructure (provided that it is paired with a billing tool like WHMCS). But most reseller hosts will sell to anybody: including people that simply have a lot of sites to find digital accommodation for and who realize that it's often a far better deal than a comparable shared hosting package.

The advantages of opting for a reseller hosting environment over a shared one is often that the resources one gets are disproportionately more generous and cost-efficient. A shared hosting account, for instance, might have a total inode limit (that's how many files and folders can be stored on the server) of, say, 100,000. A reseller hosting accounting costing just

20% more, however, might provide that same limit but for each of the ten cPanel accounts that the plan allows a user to host. So in effect you'd be paying 20% more for 1000% the resources.

WHM vs cPanel

Reseller hosting allows you to have a separate cPanel (administrative area) for each website associated with your account. And these are managed from a sort of "master" cPanel known as WHM. The servers allocated to reseller hosting typically include an operating system that offers caging — such as CloudLinux OS. This prevents the problem I mentioned in shared hosting whereby malware or other cybersecurity threats can run amok on one poorly isolated and thus vulnerable filesystem. If you're running a reseller hosting configuration and one website gets infected beyond repair you should at least in theory not have to start the other sites from scratch (but of course you should have a backup!)

Reseller hosting, despite being a very interesting and underadopted off-label option for private webmasters with large online empires, shouldn't be thought of as some sort of panacea for all users underserved by what shared hosting typically provides but who aren't yet ready to make the step up to VPS hosting, which we will look at in turn. Reseller hosting is suitable for some users but still doesn't typically afford root access to manipulate the underlying infrastructure. And there's always a risk that major hosts will stop offering it entirely: some believe there's a good chance that the chained reseller model is going to eventually give way to everybody hosting in some way or another directly from the titans of the hosting world.

If a user decides that they *are* going to need the ability to actually configure the server exactly the way they want it, to get exactly what packages they need running on the server, then they are going to need to take the next skyward step on the web hosting pecking ladder.

Virtual Private Server (VPS) Hosting

That next step up in the hosting hierarchy is called Virtual Private Server (VPS) hosting.

VPS hosting is further divided into managed and unmanaged VPS. In the latter case, as the name suggests, webmasters, like you, are responsible for managing and updating the server — and not the hosting company.

VPS is so named because the person offering it leverages the power of virtualization to abstract the underlying infrastructure (dedicated machine) on which it runs. What that means in simple terms is that, from a technical standpoint, the VPS server behaves as if it is its own physical server in a data center. Whereas in reality it is but a mere virtualized *chunk* of a bare metal (physical) server, or a cluster of them, which can be divvied up repetitively (until the cumulative chunks of virtualized computing meet the actual hardware resources on the underlying computer that is — but that's for the host to worry about, not you). This technology (virtualization) has actually existed on desktops too for quite some time so long as you have a CPU that supports the hypervisor technology needed to run it. If you'd like to see how virtualization looks and feels on a desktop, then both Oracle VirtualBox and VMWare Workstation Player can be downloaded free of charge (at the time of writing). If you're running Windows you can use them to run another operating system (say, Kali Linux) while inside Windows — and vice-versa. As with VPS machines, these behave indistinguishably (almost) from using an actual operating system installed directly onto an SSD.

Virtual machines allow a host to divide the resources at their disposal on one physical computer (or RAID server array) among many customers — as mentioned, the cumulative share of the resources apportioned to all the virtual machines simply needs to be less than that of the hardware attached to the physical machine which they are running aboard. This model allows the hosting companies to offer the service at a more affordable price than if the customers were to each lease their own computer in their server rack. Again, we see how pooling resources together creates efficiencies.

If you need a quick summation, think of VPS as a nice halfway house between shared hosting and actually owning a server that's locked up in that data center we talked about in the Nevada desert (I use the example only half-jokingly: if you trace where your public IP geolocates to you will often find that the data center your host is using is located in the most unexpected of places).

You're operating a server in a data center that looks and feels like it's your own (the resources *are* dedicated and you can manage it however you like). But if you want the real thing, and to actually directly rent some underlying hardware, then you still need something else.

And that would be:

Dedicated Hosting

The grand-daddy of many hosting offerings, dedicated hosting entails guaranteeing a client access to a dedicated server.

Unlike with VPS hosting those resources are provisioned by real physical hardware. In other words, they are not virtualized.

Dedicated hosting, unsurprisingly, is the most expensive of the commonly offered hosting options: it entails giving customers exclusive access to real, physical computers after all. But for high level stable performance for websites that receive an ongoing high flow of traffic they are still among the tools of choice.

That is, unless they opt for:

Cloud (And Elastic) Hosting

The hosting models that we have looked at so far have all had something in common even though how they are delivered differed from case to case. That is: they have entailed renting a fixed volume of hosting resources, for a fixed volume of time, from a hosting company.

However, the trend in technology these days has upended that paradigm and moved, instead, towards models that support even greater efficiency: Computing resources, infrastructure, and software should be made available only for as long as it is needed — with customers paying only for the time they use (or the queries they run, etc). This is broadly the model within which cloud hosting fits in. And that, in turn, is part of a larger revolution in technology. (It's beyond the scope of this text to explore all the variants, but the XaaS, or X as a Service revolution, continues to expand and obliterate models for charging for technology access. Things like Data as a Service, Infrastructure as a Service, Compute as a Service, and Platform as a Service are all worth becoming acquainted with — although understanding the differences between them can take time.)

With cloud hosting, a provider uses various servers to construct on-demand virtualized "servers" which can then be used by customers. But they need only be used as required on a sort of pay as you go basis. This type of hosting is highly elastic and scalable by design — more resources and instances can be added as needs expand allowing companies to scale up and down as their computing requirements expand and contract. In fact these days, the very act of managing infrastructure is increasingly being conducted automatically by orchestration engines. Serverless cloud architectures and Kubernetes are at the forefront of this advance. This type of 'hosting' configuration is more commonly used by professional technology companies and those on the enterprise level of the scale we delineated towards the start of this chapter. Ever wondered what kind of hosting an operation the size of eBay or CNN uses to power its websites? You can bet that it isn't a budget shared hosting plan — and that a board meeting of the technical team hasn't been convened to discuss whether or not the company should spin up another server instance to provision the space that they need in the cloud.

The Onwards Journey

At this stage of our journey we've succeeded in staking out our territory on the internet — through the grand act of purchasing a domain name which is really, in essence, just a sort of temporary deed to an alphanumeric file pattern that makes it easier to access the web infrastructure that we're going to build at that URL.

We've found somewhere to actually store the files and databases that we're going to need to make things work online — by finding a hosting provider and identifying a type of hosting that is best positioned to meet our needs right now.

The final thing which we might want to put is in place is an uptime monitor. This is a service that will periodically check our website and send us an email alert if it goes down. There are both free and paid versions available and the difference is usually simply that the paid version which check to see if our site is on the internet at a more frequent interval.

Now we're ready to go and make things happen on the internet.

In Summary:

- Buying a 'domain' allows you to rent an entry, for a period of time, in a system that helps users direct alphanumeric names to internet protocol (IP) addresses. You can think of it like digital feudalism. The domain registrar is the entity you buy a domain name from. And there's usually nothing stopping you from using a separate company to manage a domain and host with so long as you make sure that nameservers, a type of DNS record, are configured correctly.
- The files, databases and other components that make a website 'work' need some computer to live on in the internet. This is so that they can serve content to those that want to access them. Those computers, in turn, are called servers. And hosting companies allows users to rent access to them.
- These are various types of hosting available for websites of different sizes.
- Shared hosting is the starting point and the cheapest option — although there are a number of technical deficiencies you should be aware of and it's not the best option for sites with high levels of traffic (most importantly because server resources are not guaranteed but rather shared dynamically with other tenants on the server).
- You can subscribe to reseller hosting without actually being a reseller. Reseller hosts typically offer caging and isolation — so that there's no risk of cross-infection if one website gets hacked.

89

- VPS is the next notch up in the hosting hierarchy. Like desktop hardware virtualization, this abstracts underlying computing resources to divide physical resources between users. This allows hosting companies to offer the technology at a lower price point than dedicated servers for comparable features. For users, the experience is typically no different than owning 'bare metal' hardware. The operating system can be configured as required. VPS usually exists in both managed and unmanaged variants.
- Dedicated servers entail actually owning a physical server with real hardware. As in — an actual server sitting in a rack in a data center somewhere that is provisioned just for your usage.
- Cloud hosting is another concept entirely, typically favored by technology companies and enterprises — especially those offering SaaS products with often rapidly changing infrastructural requirements. In this concept, the underlying hardware isn't even fixed but can rather be provisioned upon demand and billed to users on a pay as you go basis. This makes it easier for large companies to scale up and scale down use as their needs change. This concept, of elasticity, also fits within a larger technical trend of paying for resources as they are required rather than for a fixed time period: 'X'-as-a-Service. There are many variants.

3. BUILDING (ON THE INTERNET)

Furnishing our digital home

Now that we have some online real estate to call our own, it's time to begin developing whatever we need to market ourselves to the world as a freelancer. For most people the centerpoint of that infrastructure is going to be what's commonly referred to as a website.

If you're feeling a little bit mentally jarred at this point, that's okay. The opening two chapters were about as technical as this book is going to get — and is close to where the limits of my own understanding of these concepts lie. I wanted to make sure that I properly explained the products and relationships that connect the components needed to actually put things on the internet in the first place. So that when it comes time to renew your domain — or upgrade your hosting — you can understand roughly what you're shelling more of your hard-earned cash in exchange for. And as I mentioned, if you *do* opt for an all-in-one solution (and, as I said, I don't recommend that you do if you have long term scalability in mind) these components will be hidden from your view but likely managed automatically under the hood by your provider. But it's still good to understand that they exist and why they do.

Now that we're the proud owner of hosting services somewhere, we have a server (if it's shared - preconfigured) to begin doing things with.

Before we get going with building an actual website on it, let's do some basic housekeeping to get our hosting environment nicely set up and ready for putting things in place on.

Installing an SSL Certificate

You've probably noticed that just about every website that you visits these days (in Google Chrome) has a little padlock icon preceding the URL. If you haven't noticed it, then it looks like this.

This symbol is automatically added to the omnibox (in Google Chrome) whenever the browser successfully verifies that the website has a valid SSL/TLS certificate installed (more commonly these are still simply known as 'SSL certs'). If you're using a self-signed certificate, which is a sort of DIY approach to SSL certifications, then you might run into some problems with this. But as many hosting companies offer unlimited free SSL certificates these days that should be more of an academic concern.

Whatever UI feature a browser uses to highlight the fact, websites bearing an SSL certification can use the HTTPS protocol, rather than HTTP, to send traffic to and from the webserver which they are hosted on. The 'S' in HTTPS stands for 'secure' — and it means roughly what it says on the tin: HTTPS ensures that traffic is secured between the website and the viewer.

Nowadays, you can effectively consider an SSL certificate to be an essential prerequisite to gaining any internet browser's trust — and yes, even many that aren't of a technical inclination (increasingly, browsers warn users when the pages they are visiting are not being served over HTTPS, letting them know, in no uncertain terms, that they are not 'secure'.) This is particularly true if you're planning on selling anything online —

in which case providing this technology is absolutely essential. Therefore it's worth taking a few minutes to review whether your hosting package came with SSL certificates for all your domains. If it did, have they been automatically installed correctly? If not, is there something you can do to install them? If necessary, you can usually liaise with your hosting company's technical support team (this is what they are there for). But usually this is something that should work out of the box.

Setting Up Email

The cPanel provided with virtually every shared hosting environment these days actually contains a veritable suite full of tools which should be enough to enable the user to configure email addresses and send and receive email correspondence.

Most hosts' cPanels look slightly different (some hosts lock down functionalities that would otherwise be available). But most nevertheless contain what could be regarded as a common core set of features.

Besides locking down features, some hosts may restrict usage limits on the features that are provided. Both these techniques are typically done in order to try upsell you on higher hosting tiers which usually lift these artificial restrictions. A host may, for instance, enforce arbitrary limits as to how may email addresses — or forwards — a user can configure. Or offer various limits with various tiers. Sometimes, this can seem like nickel and diming. Thankfully, when it comes to choosing a host, there are many options — just do a little bit of research to make sure that the source you're getting information or reviews from is a legitimate one and not an affiliate marketing operation that makes every vendor sound great in order to try get you to sign up with them (if you didn't figure out the business logic at work: the site operators get a kickback; therefore, offering truthful information may not always be in their best interests.)

Setting up email addresses in cPanel is actually very straightforward and playing around with the features for ten minutes or so should be enough to understand the majority of capabilities on offer.

cPanel's Built In Email Features

After purchasing hosting most users assume that connecting the domain to G Suite is the essential next order of business. This is not, in fact, the case.

The email features presented in an average host's cPanel are actually more than enough to do business with. G Suite and Office 365 may be excellent products but they are *not* required in order to operate personalized email addresses in the format email@yourdomain.com (however, you can add an address you own *to* your existing Gmail account if it's more convenient for you to do so. We'll cover how presently).

The following whistle stop tour is simply intended to highlight some of the most important email features within cPanel — and to offer notes about how you might wish to use them in concert with your existing online infrastructure. As with the exact features present in cPanel, User interface (UI) verbiage and the nomenclature of these menu items may differ slightly depending upon the host that you have chosen to use.

- **Email accounts:** This tool can be used to create email addresses and set and update passwords for them. You can also bring up the connection initiation screen from this list which provides the settings you will need to use in order to access these addresses from a third party client (ie, by not accessing them through the webmail feature of your host). If you wish to receive email on a third party app then you'll need to use the details for the outgoing server (SMTP). On the other side of the equation, for inbound email, the modern protocol is called IMAP (POP should be avoided unless you have no choice). Nowadays there's also a great feature to email configuration instructions to anybody that needs them directly from within the configuration screen. If you're setting up an email address for another member of your team, for instance, after provisioning an address for them, and setting their password, you can email them the configuration instructions. The email is automatically formatted and should contain all the information they need — minus the password — to get the account working with any kind of email client. You just have to input their email address to the field and click the send button.

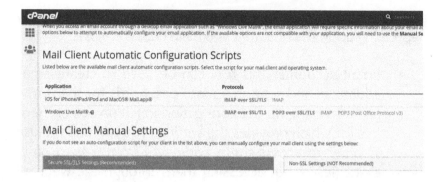

- **Forwarders:** Commonly, as a freelancer, you will want to continue operating from your personal Gmail address, but put a more professional-looking branded email on your business cards, website, and other pieces of marketing collateral. That's the type of email address that ends in your domain name. Thankfully these can be very easily configured. You can use a branded email address within Gmail itself: simply set up a forwarder from you@yourdomain.com to you@gmail.com; then add you@yourdomain.com as a sending account in Gmail, inputting the credentials from the email configuration screen above; and finally click on the verification code when the confirmation email links back to you. Alternatively you can simply opt to receive communications directed to your vanity address (you@yourdomain.com) at your Gmail (you@gmail.com) — but continue the correspondence from your Gmail (in this second scenario we are simply not using the branded email as a sending address within Gmail). In order to do this, you can simply rig up a forwarder to your Gmail. If you sign up for one of the online collaboration suites that we'll discuss in the next chapter, covering SaaS, then you can brand your email and send from the familiar interfaces that these operators provide.

- **Default address:** This is also known as a catchall. And if you want unrouted email (email to your domain sent to a non-existent address) to route to a specific inbox rather than fail with an error, then this is where that setting is configured. This can be used to good effect in organization systems — or to spoof the existence of non-existent email addresses (those you haven't created an account for) when using third party email marketing tools that confirm email addresses simply by sending a verification email to them.
- **Spam filtering:** This bit is important. If you're going to be piping on your correspondence to a Gmail address then it's best to completely disable the spam filtering options in cPanel. This is because Gmail, and indeed most webmail tools, have their own built-in spam filtering. Filtering things twice, rather than providing enhanced protection against spam, actually just increases the likelihood that legitimate messages will accidentally get caught up in the inappropriate dragnet created. Gmail and most webmail clients also have native whitelisting functionality and automatic rules can be configured by setting up automated filters. These are not intended to be used with email that has already been filtered at source and then forwarded. For that reason, it makes the most sense to pipe the mail from your cPanel address unprocessed by a spam filter and then let Gmail organize received messages into communications that it believes to be spam and those which it determines are from legitimate senders. If you determine, for instance, that Gmail is incorrect, the spam filter can be reconfigured accordingly. If there were another tool filtering the messages before they

were forwarded to Gmail this setting change may not have any effect. Just don't forget to disable the various spam filtering options in cPanel — these are typically enabled by default.

After configuring the above settings, you should have all the functionality you might need to either access your inboxes from a desktop-based client or else to run your email "on top of" another system such as G Suite or Gmail (so to speak).

As above, small configuration changes will effect how, exactly, this system works.

For instance, the forwarding option you use will determine whether emails being forwarded from your cPanel account to your Gmail (or other externally managed address) are merely routed on or stored on the hosting company's server and *then* processed:

- If you simply set up forwarders from *you@yourdomain.com* to *you@gmail.com* the messages will not be stored on the mail server at yourdomain.com as they pass through on their way to their ultimate destination (your Gmail inbox).
- If, however, you create an inbox for *you@yourdomain.com and* set up a forwarder to forward email to *you@yourdomain.com* automatically onto *you@gmail.com* then the email messages will be stored *both* on the mail server at yourdomain.com, which is managed by your host, and in your Gmail.

It's important to also check the storage limits for each inbox that you configure on your email server. And if you're doing a lot of emailing and the email storage limit that your host provides is not particularly generous then it may make sense to go with one of the above configurations over the other. If you're engaging in email marketing at any volume then it also makes sense to look up the SMTP limits that your web hosting company imposes — most will specify a maximum number of emails that can be sent per day and/or per hour and document these somewhere in their support resources. If you've edited your mail DNS records (MX entries) and are managing your email through an external service such as G Suite then clearly your hosting company's sending limits are irrelevant — as your email is now being hosted and parsed by Google. However Google, in turn, will stipulate its own sending limits — which we will look at in more detail later when we're talking about marketing email delivery services and why you might also want to use one.

Setting up Cloudflare

While we're still at the stage of configuring basic online infrastructure it's worth taking a look at a service called Cloudflare.

Cloudflare acts as something of an intermediary between users' websites (and the servers associated with them) and the outside internet. If you've ever tried to reach a website that is protected by Cloudflare and been presented with a schematic showing where the connection choked (usually between Cloudflare and the destination server, which was down at the time that you tried to make the connection) then you should have a good intuitive understanding of how exactly the service works.

Cloudflare fulfills a number of very important functionalities all of which might potentially be useful to you as a webhost (even if all you are hosting is a simple portfolio websites):

- It masks the identity of your servers (assuming you let it — check that your proxy settings are on orange. If they are not the DNS requests are being passed *through* Cloudflare but the proxying isn't happening).
- It speeds up the delivery of your content by providing caching.
- You can create page and firewall rules directly on Cloudflare — blocking traffic from a certain country, for instance.

Because Cloudflare sits between the visiting public and your web infrastructure operated by your hosting company there's even more to it than that. You can serve Google Analytics code or even create popups by using Cloudflare plugins, for instance. But — as a free service (on its basic plan) — it, at the very least, can be used to upgrade the security and speed of your website. (If you change hosts and own a multitude of websites, Cloudflare will also make the process a lot easier. Rather than having to update nameservers with every domain registrar all DNS records can be updated in bulk from your Cloudflare account).

Once Cloudflare is installed on your domain — and you have updated the name-servers at your domain registrar to tunnel traffic through its network — then this is also the place where you will be updating and maintaining DNS records (rather than in cPanel). These DNS records, as we covered previously, are the entries that tell those trying to access your resources where to find them. They effectively create relationships between public IP addresses and alphanumeric strings. If you sign up for an email marketing service that requires that you create an SPF TXT record to assist with deliverability and authentication, for instance, then this will be the place where you will need to create, or update, the records.

Building a Website

We now have the basics of our web infrastructure set up. But of course there's one thing that we're missing — the star of the show! — and that's the website which this whole infrastructure has been provisioned to host.

In case your motivation is already waning let me tell you that we're only four lines of rudimentary markdown away from bringing a fully functional website to life which you can show customers by directing them to yourdomain.com. Well, if you'll allow me some artistic license about what constitutes a 'website' that is.

You could copy the following into a text editor:

```
<html>
<title>Welcome to my homepage!</title>
<h1>Welcome to my cool new site!</h1>
</html>
```

Now save the file as index.html.

If you were to navigate to the file manager in cPanel, move to the root directory of whatever domain you'd like to build the website at, and then upload this file — every visitor that accessed your website would receive that enthusiastic message. And — because we added a <title> tag the tab's title would even display the page title too. Congratulations, you've put a website on the internet!

I'm going to assume, however, that you're seeking to do something a little bit more sophisticated than build a website that contains just six words of texts welcoming visitors to a website that doesn't do anything other than ... display a welcome message to visitors.

You're probably going to want some dynamic content (for which you'll need a database and PHP files to dynamically query it for content), some splashes of color (for which you'll need CSS), and some scripts that do fancy things such as help you find out who's accessing your website at this current moment — and from where in the world.

Before you say *"hang on, isn't that what Wordpress does?"* allow me to draw your attention towards another great service which will make your life as a webmaster much less strenuous.

Softaculous

Softaculous is a one click web script installer which comes with many hosting packages. And before we go into exactly what it does, let's first understand the concept of server software.

You're undoubtedly familiar with the type of software that you install on your computer. Think of the Word document processing tool. Now think about how software like this is typically installed.

Nowadays, and since the passage of the CD era, one typically does that by downloading some sort of installation file from a website, opening the file by clicking on the file that was downloaded, and then following the system prompts until the progress bar proudly announces that the process is complete. Now think about what's happening under the hood. As that progress bar is shifting right, the program is installing and configuring itself on your operating system — doing everything convenient to make itself accessible to you (such as creating entries in your operating system's menu navigation tree so that you have an icon to click on whenever you need to run it.)

Just as there are pieces of software written for desktop environments that expect to be installed, and run, on a desktop computing environment, there are pieces of software that are written to run on a server on the cloud.

The main difference, technically, will be that the graphical user interface (GUI) which the server programs provide will be piped over a web browser with two ends to it: an administrative end where you can configure changes and set things up (the backend) and an attractive looking website which those accessing the site see assuming that they don't input the special administrative URL (the frontend). You're already probably familiar with at least one such script — Wordpress —

but in reality there are plenty more. Many of these, like Wordpress, are free and open source.

Unlike desktop software, server programs don't provide a "program" that is designed to be accessed from a programs menu as such. For the simple reason (as we will see later) that servers don't typically expect to provide a graphical desktop environment of that nature at all. They're there to serve content over the internet for access in a desktop machine - not to be directly interacted with, for entertainment, by an end user.

The installation process for server-side scripts is typically a little bit more involved than when you're installing things on your desktop. But — because I want to point out how worthwhile these tools can be — they are not something that I want to gloss over either.

Installing Server Scripts: The Manual Way

We just sketched out what the typical user experience for installing a desktop piece of software might look like. So now let's do the same for programs — namely scripts — that are intended to run on servers.

Typically, to install a software script, one would download the latest version of the software from the maintainer's website directly to the web hosting server. And let's refresh on what that server is. In its most basic form a web hosting server (the type we looked at in the previous chapter) is a remote machine nestled in some data center. That's almost certainly a good description for the computer that's serving your web pages to the public. It is a called a "headless" machine because — unlike the computer that might be in front of you as you read this — it doesn't have a desktop environment and therefore graphical user interfaces (GUIs — you can think of these as programs). GUIs are the things that make interacting with programs as easy as moving a mouse around some pixel space and in order to change settings, take actions, receive content, and generally interface with the program.

The initial stages of installing server programs, by contrast to our desktop experience, would typically be done over the command line — and usually after using something called an SSH tunnel to securely connect from a local machine (say, your laptop) to the remote server within a terminal. We would then typically use commands like 'curl' or 'wget' to download a package from the internet. Typing words like 'curl' and 'get' into a terminal and then adding operators is actually using something called Command Line Interfaces (CLIs). These are programs that are intended to be accessed over a terminal — to be contrasted with the GUIs that we just learned about. GUIs typically also have CLIs that aim to offer more or less the same set of functionalities — but to provide them over a terminal. However plenty of CLIs have no GUIs at all. These days, it's mostly Linux users that spend time using CLIs on the desktop. But they remain the typical way of interfacing with a server and installing packages and programs from the internet onto them — particularly when the desired server package provides no graphical frontend over the internet (contrast this case with cPanel or Wordpress which are pieces of server software that *do* have web browser accessed graphical interfaces).

After downloading the server program the user might need to consult the installation documentation, manually create a MySQL database (which allows users to create, save, store, and retrieve information), ensure that the package has been given the correct access permissions on the server, and then edit some configuration files to connect the two together.

Phew!

Even though there are plenty of scripts like Wordpress that make extensive use of graphical browser-served frontends to make the process a lot easier, the pure terminal-centric process outlined above is still commonplace. It's worth getting a feel for it in case you *do* ever need to carry it out if there is an open source script that Softaculous does *not* have in its library which you would like to install.

Installing Server Software With Softaculous

However, if the script *is* in Softaculous's library, it makes the task of installing server software childishly simple by comparison to the example I outlined above.

Firstly, you need to find the script that you like from the Softaculous library. Then you click on the 'install now' button and wait a few seconds. After a few seconds have elapsed the browser will provide you with a link to the program that you have just installed as well as a confirmation email that contains a link to the backend — which will usually be termed the administrative URL. Everything — downloading the latest version of the program, creating the database, and connecting the two — will have taken place seamlessly in the backend in the blink of an eye. It's done — and you're good to go.

Wordpress vs. Other CMSs vs. DIY Website Builders

At this stage you may want to go ahead and install Wordpress using Softaculous — or some other one click type installer that your webhost has provisioned on your hosting account.

If you're a freelancer and you're not using an all-in-one builder than it's fair to say that it's the Content Management System (CMS) of choice — although Drupal and Joomla both remain popular options and are sometimes the better options for websites that are not built around the framework of a weblog (these are just a little more difficult to learn with Drupal commonly thought of as being harder than Joomla).

If you're looking to run an e-commerce website, to sell things online, then a script such as Magento (open source) or Shopify (SaaS website frontend; monthly) would be better options, even though the popular WooCommerce plugin allows you to add e-commerce functionalities on top of Wordpress. CMS scripts that are optimized for e-commerce will typically contain features such as inventory management and payment gateways, among others. And many other scripts specialized for various purposes — from hosting your own bulletin boards to Wikipedia lookalikes — exist too. There's no need to pick one: it's possible to run various applications on different parts of a URL, or to put some services on subdomains (x.yourdomain.com). At the biggest level of scale, companies even run different parts of their website from web infrastructure that is geographically separated.

Despite my encouragement to actually build a website (whether with a CMS or by hand) you may, of course, choose to go down the route of using an all in-one website builder to handle all aspects of rolling out your new website (and many providers really take care of everything — including the domain name purchase, hosting, and designing and maintaining the site in one fixed price). Wix, Squarespace, and Weblium are three commonly used platforms for this purpose (among many options). Website builders allow you to get a web presence on the internet extremely quickly — in time for dinner, even. But their advantages in terms of easy setup are matched by some negatives that it's worth knowing about before you get too excited by the sales pitch. For one, you won't get to learn about how to update DNS records (just kidding - that's not a real disadvantage). But on a serious note, by tying up all aspects of managing your site with one provider, you will (often) find that you won't be able to upgrade between hosting tiers, change to a different domain registrar, or things of that nature. In other words: get ready for a serious case of vendor lock. Additionally, the type of features that you can use will be limited to the vendor has chosen to offer. You will often find that these tools are rather aggressive about upselling use tiers for the same reason. Finally, these websites are really intended for small businesses. Naturally, for freelancers starting out, this is probably a good fit — which explains their popularity among thing user base. Much of the following information about cloud-hosted services is also not applicable in the kind of environment that point and click website builders typically offer. You'll get space to build a drag and drop website. Perhaps a couple of tools to build a couple of contact forms and tweak some SEO elements like page metatitles and metadescriptions. And not a whole lot of anything else. Whether you like the thought of going with this option and then switching (if needs be) down the road or you'd rather put in the hard work of building something more professional and scalable from the outset really depends on which side of the "do things that don't (or do) scale" debate that you're on. I'm a scalability and let's start planning for bigger and better things kind of guy — to an extreme extent that probably hinders my ability to just get up and running quickly. So I'm not necessarily stating that that's the right approach. If you do go with the website builder approach then you'll probably want to skip over some of the information in the chapter on SaaS — although it might be helpful to know anyway. Pick what you think works best for you and whatever aligns in the tidiest manner possible with your medium to long term growth plan.

Having now set up the basics in a shared hosting environment, like email and a CMS, we'll move on to the additional applications you might want to run in the cloud in order to run your business as efficiently as possible.

As we do so we'll mention open source alternatives where there are noteworthy options that you might want to keep in mind when evaluating what tool is best suited to your needs.

Unless otherwise stated these are free web scripts that can be installed almost effortlessly using Softaculous and which — at least during your early days — can help realize you substantial savings by cutting down on your Software as a Software (SaaS) budget by avoiding monthly subscription costs.

Let's take a look at those. And look a little bit more closely about what the whole concept of the 'cloud' actually means.

Wordpress vs. Other CMSs

In summary:

- cPanel is the suite of tools you'll be using to manage basic aspects of your webhosting experience. Like many of the other tools we will be looking at shortly it is a type of cloud hosted software provisioned on your web server by your host.

- Almost all hosts actually come with a set of tools to set up an email system — although the webmail clients they work with will likely seem rudimentary to you by comparison with modern standards. These tools can be manipulated in cPanel.
- If you want to use the branded email your host provides without the help of an external service provider such as G Suite (but don't want to give up on the convenience of accessing your email from a commercial webmail client like Gmail) then you can set up catchalls and pipe on email to your Gmail address.
- If you're already a Gmail user, you can even add an address @yourdomain.com and send and receive from it directly from within your Gmail. This allows you to send and receive using the email service that your ISP provides — without having to do so from an unattractive interface. This can be set up in a couple of minutes by following a few steps.
- Cloudflare is a third party service that is definitely worth considering. It sits between your website and the internet. It's a free tool (on its basic tier) and has many useful functionalities including masking the IP address of the various servers you use to deliver web traffic to those requesting it.
- There are software programs that can be installed onto a server just as there are programs that be installed onto a local computer. It's just that the process is typically a bit more difficult. The programs are usually CLIs rather than GUIs and do not expect the user to have a display interface available to directly interact with them. This is because they are installed on servers which are typically headless environments. In many cases, however, they do drive output to a web browser. This makes interacting with them almost as easy as following a local desktop installation process.
- The Wordpress CMS is an example of one of these — although there are many others.

- Softaculous is a one click installer that aims to simplify the installation of serverside scripts. It takes all the hard work out of installing programs on your server — although its library does not contain every server program out there and it focuses on those that are widely used and stable.
- Server software typically has two 'ends' to it: a backend for setting administrative configurations and a frontend that is presented to the end-user.
- Many server scripts are free and open-source. For this reason alone, it's worth checking out what's on offer as they might be able to provide the same functionality as SaaS tools — for a fraction of the price (if, indeed, for any).
- You can also install server scripts that aren't in Softaculous's library — although you'll likely have to grapple with some CLIs and your host's server configuration will have to be suitable for the desired script(s).

4. PRODUCT ASSEMBLY (AND SAAS)
All the things we'll need on the cloud

Our journey so far has been a holistic one of sorts.

We've moved from the ground up — starting with how to get a home office provisioned with a decent internet connection; we've looked at how to choose a computer that will be best suited to your needs as a freelancer; and we've delved into what things might make your home office a more productive, and ergonomic, environment to work in.

Turning to the online world, we've looked at the nuts and bolts of what's required to keep a website running on the internet starting with buying a domain name; we configured our bare-bones but functional cPanel host-issued email to send and received 'branded' email from; and we've used a one-click installation tool such as Softaculous to install a couple of open source scripts on our server such as Wordpress. This, in turn, has given us the firepower to actually do useful things with the online infrastructure that we set up — like build an impressive looking website to show to potential clients. It may not be the most advanced setup that has ever been created. But it's on the internet. And it (hopefully) works.

At this point we're ready to go ahead and build a website. A Wordpress site would be fine or we could even hand over FTP (file management) credentials to a web development firm and let them build us something completely from scratch. It's up to us. And likely the decision will depend on the budget that we have at our disposal.

However, and whatever option we choose in that decision-making process, it's highly unlikely that a website is going to be *all* the technology that we are going to require in order to run a thriving freelance business online — at least one which is ready to scale up.

How to build a fantastic website that wows your prospective clients isn't going to be covered here: That depends, instead, on the platform you choose to build on as well as many other factors such as the functionalities you'd like to see it have and the design you're aiming for. And if you've gone the 'all in one' route then of course much of the foregoing may not have been applicable to you at all.

So let's leave that process aside. And move on instead to the other technical services that you might be requiring in order to accelerate your quest towards freelance world domination.

To do that, we're going to take a look at all the bits and pieces that we might need in order to round out our stack — which, as we said in the introduction, is a shorthand for the series of technologies and integrations that we're going to be putting together in order to make magic happen online. And, as promised, I'll be making reference, where possible, to potential open source replacements for some of the Software as a Service (SaaS) tools mentioned here.

We'll be taking a look at some of the components that we might need one by one. But first: let's understand a little bit more about this mysterious entity we've mentioned quite a few times so far throughout this text. The one that might be in the sky. Or beneath the ground. That nebulous home of so much modern computing simply called 'the cloud'.

What's The Cloud? (And Why It Makes Sense To Adopt A Cloud-First Approach)

These days it makes sense for most businesses to be a cloud-first organization.

And If you're confused about what the 'cloud' is then there's no need to be — We've literally just deployed some resources 'on the cloud' in the last chapter.

But what is the cloud and how did it wind up with such a curious name you might be wondering? Let's look at its history to find out.

Why The Cloud Is Called The Cloud

When network engineers used to plot out network diagrams, a cloud would be drawn to represent the resources that 'lived' aboard online infrastructure — just as we have just set up some resources, like a website, on top of our web hosting server. In pure networking terms these online applications could be thought of as an abstraction —they're just lines of code in some server at the end of the day rather than a physical entity, or piece of infrastructure, somewhere along the network. But it's these same lines of code that form the basis for many modern day businesses and allow them to impress prospects with nicely designed websites.

In more practical terms, when we talk about the cloud these days we're really simply talking about accessing data that is stored in a computer that we're not actively managing — to contrast with one that we are such as, say, our desktop computer. We could drill down further into the differences between public, private, and hybrid clouds. But ownership is not the critical factor — so saying that the cloud is simply "somebody else's computer" is not true in all cases even if the refrain has developed as a sort of common shorthand (companies might deploy offsite private clouds but own the data center that houses them for instance). Neither is the location the defining factor. A cloud could be on-site and private although most clouds that we're talking about here are off-site (they're managed in a data center) and public (we don't have exclusive access to the servers contained there — we just get user access to an application that they happen to be running and which appealed to us enough that we determined we wanted access to). An easier definition might rather be that the cloud is a server, or a collection of them, that is accessed over the internet. As a server (or a datacenter) its job is to provide access to that data, or those applications, on demand. And typically it is available from anywhere on the planet that has an internet connection which is not blocked by its firewall.

Cloud computing has revolutionized the technology landscape over the past decade. Most businesses processes that could previously only be done locally can these days easily be migrated to comparable systems on the cloud — in time (in some cases!) for lunch. A vibrant ecosystem has thus grown up to help businesses expedite this process and ensure successful cloud deployments. There are scores of consultancies that specialize solely in helping small businesses with so-called legacy-to-cloud migrations. Which is why I say that, unless you have a strong countervailing reason, it makes sense to take a cloud-first approach from the very outset.

Some Legacy to Cloud Examples

An accounting system that is stored on the manager's computer, for instance, is a common local system. But it could just as easily be reprovisioned on a cloud accounting software

— the manager would simply store information directly on the internet (which is really a server computer in some data center managed by a SaaS provider) rather than directly on his or her personal computer.

These days most mainstream cloud software is provided via a Software as a Service (SaaS) model. And the advantages are significant. Because the computer storing his/her accounting information is professionally managed and constantly accessible over the internet, the accounting manager can retrieve, update, or modify the accounting information from any computer with an internet connection: whether the computer used to do so is a Windows machine in the office, or a Mac halfway up Mount Everest, is completely immaterial.

Operating system agnosticism is thus another fringe benefit of cloud computing worth mentioning in passing. In particular, Linux users long used to experiencing compatibility issues with Windows and their platform of choice can take advantage of accessing software which simply requires a web browser to access (and web browses are, almost without exception cross-platform on the desktop).

Keep Your Own Data

There is one caveat to my support of cloud computing, however. And that is that I think whenever you are storing your data on somebody else's computer you should, ideally, go to pains to make sure that you periodically keep your own copy.

SaaS simply means that the software is hosted by the software vendor (on a public cloud). And users pay a monthly subscription in order to retain access to the technology. Clearly many — even freelancers — would consider it prudent to keep a copy of all mission-critical data that is being entrusted to third party providers in systems that they cannot directly manage.

There are potential privacy and compliance for some to countenance too (we'll cover these in more detail in the backups chapter). Some governmental and large organizations are not able, or reluctant, to use the cloud for certain applications for this very reason — although amazingly AWS has developed highly secured versions of its cloud computing infrastructure that have been used by governmental and law enforcement agencies.

Despite these limitations surrounding privacy and non-ownership of the software being accessed, I would strongly contend that it makes sense for most freelancers to take a cloud-first approach when it comes to any tool or software that might benefit their business.

The software, despite not being one's own, can be accessed from anywhere; it's continuously improved upon and managed by professionals; and the risks to one's data can be mitigated by moving it periodically onsite if so desired.

Common SaaS Products (And Why You Might Need Them)

An Online Collaboration Tool: G Suite or Office 365

Now that we've clarified a little what the cloud is and why it makes more sense for most freelancers to host as many of their business applications as possible on it, let's take a look at some of the most commonly adopted cloud tools.

These are the basics that almost every freelancer that wants to get going in a modern way will probably want to arm him or herself with.

The first tool is an **online collaboration suite**. Two major providers dominate the marketplace at the freelancer and SMB-friendly level of scale — Google's G-suite and Microsoft's Office 365 — although there are smaller contenders such as Zoho that offer similar functionalities for an often cheaper price point.

If you've spent any time editing a Google Document or using Gmail — and I'm guessing that you've done both plenty of times! — then you understand the concept at work here. It's really simply the concept that we've just laid out (cloud software offered as a service). Google provisions email management and desktop publishing software in the cloud, makes it available for anybody that pays, and all that's left for users to do is sign up for an account and pay a monthly or yearly subscription in order to gain access to it. By contrast with desktop software, users don't need to install any programs in order to get it to run — they just need to point their web browsers at the URL the software is hosted on (at the time of writing, for instance, drive.google.com for Google Drive). The software runs on Google's servers rather than on their local computer. It's continuously updated and maintained by Google (with many updates evading users' attention entirely). But if users want to pull their own data out they will need to typically follow some kind of procedure to do so, assuming that the feature is offered (at the time of writing, Google's main user-focused tool for this purpose is known as Google Takeouts).

G Suite (or even the free Google platform) is much more than just cloud file storage, of course. Both G Suite and Office 365 are full fledged online productivity and collaboration services. In addition to providing webmail (and email), the services provide the aforementioned office collaboration suites, calendar management, contact /address book management, and more.

There are noteworthy differences between the Google and Microsoft products — and others. But the uniting thread that ties all the different "apps" together is that they're software programs that live in the cloud — even if they sync with local devices (consider, for instance, Google Contacts syncing with a user's cellphone). Together these two suites enable millions of freelancers the world over to run their businesses much more efficiently.

Cloud File Storage

Gmail (free), G Suite, and Office 365 provide online file storage as *part* of their offerings.

By way of contrast, there are a number of cloud service providers whose sole offering *is* consumer-oriented cloud file storage (we'll look at object cloud storage in the backups chapter). This list includes pCloud, Dropbox, and Box.com. The cloud storage providers vary in terms of the amount of free storage space that they provide, the price of their paid plans, the kind of version control features they offer, and the desktop tools and how they work. (Although the use-case is starkly different — managing code repositories rather than files and folders — Git is a program for collaboratively managing code repositories and working with rigorous version control. The tools which file-sharing focused platforms offer are usually not optimized to manage changes in the same exacting manner as Git. But it's worth nevertheless checking out what each offers. Git is a sort of gold standard for version control and it's worth becoming familiar with the tool — and code hosting platforms that use the Git technology to allow users to push updates to — in general).

The cloud hosting tools also differ in terms of how they interact with local filesystems. While some, for instance, mount to the local filesystem as a virtual drive — requiring almost no direct local storage space to make this happen — others are sync clients and might require extensive storage on the user's computer to duplicate the storage in the cloud (and if the size of the cloud storage volume exceeds that which is available locally users might have to compromise on what data they can sync with the cloud).

Open source alternative: Owncloud is an open source script which can be deployed on a web server. It provides similar functionality to that of most cloud-based file storage systems including an attractive frontend. Installing Owncloud also automatically installs a WebDAV server — a protocol which can be used to transfer in and out files programatically from other devices. Servers for serving a calendar management and contact system are available too.

Customer Relationship Management (CRM)

And now we come to the CRM.

This is one tool that you might not have come across or used before when interfacing with cloud tools in a personal capacity. So I'll explain in a bit more depth exactly what it does and why you might want to use one.

We discussed, in the introduction, how business development as a freelancer is ideally a multifaceted endeavor. How many freelancers are able to sustain themselves solely by tapping into their professional network of current or past clients — or work colleagues. About how others, though, have to engage in a bit more grunt work in order to get the first prospects to sign along the dotted line and turn into paying clients. And that grunt work is the sometimes thankless but often necessary business of prospecting for leads.

The Need For Constant Sales and Marketing

How to run your own sales and marketing is obviously, again, well beyond the scope of this work — as well as the parameters of my expertise. Beyond simple outbound sales prospecting there's an entire world of inbound marketing to explore — as well as specific assets and tactics, like using lead magnets, that a lot of the technology mentioned here should enable you to do. Play around with the features of any tool you're using to understand exactly what it can and cannot do.

Although the foregoing is true, there's one piece of advice that I can't resist throwing in parenthetically. And that's that freelancers should — ideally — be marketing themselves *all of the time*. That means that even when your book of business is bursting at the seams and you can't even begin to envision how you might be able to handle more work if it came your way you should *still* keep your foot on the pedal. (And if you need a quick answer to how to handle the conundrum of how you could handle more work than you have capacity to take on then, you guessed it, outsourcing is the common recommendation.) Doing this involves always building pipeline — drumming up interest in your services and having exploratory/initial conversations with those that might need your services next business quarter (or the one after or the one after that). If you do this right you should have a slow trickle of leads constantly percolating into the later stages of your funnel. And, as a freelancer, there's nothing like a strong flow of potential customers to help you sleep better at night.

Why You Need CRM

If you understand this then you can appreciate the need for a Customer Relationship Management (CRM) tool.

If you're engaged in outbound lead generation on an ongoing basis then you're going to be writing the same thing. Over and over and over again. Will you hire me please? Here's my portfolio. Here's my website. Did you see the last reminder I sent about that invoice that was due 52 days ago? And many similar communications.

CRMs aren't just tools that make popping prepopulated templates into emails quick and easy (although they can certainly be used to do that well.) And for best results you should carefully tailor each outbound communication. But still, common sense does not have to be sacrificed in the name of doing things by the book — and there's no reason why you shouldn't be using basic text skeletons, or text snippets, to make the job of writing those emails that little bit simpler. Almost all CRMs contain functionalities to enable users to do this.

Technically-speaking, CRM is actually a philosophy rather than a distinct software product — although these days it's come to essentially mean the latter and the purpose of CRM-the-software products is really to facilitate the smooth operation of CRM-the-concept (which encourages better and more effective managing of customers by businesses and freelancers such as you).

I've always thought that CRM is actually a bit of a misnomer, actually. Because just about every CRM I have ever used has included a default taxonomy that allowed for tracking both *leads* — those that have not converted to paying customers yet — as well as *clients* (those that have). And in the world of sales, where the various stages of the prospect journey are tracked and conceived of through the construct of a funnel, the nomenclature employed by most CRMs to distinguish between different entity types is in fact designed to mirror quite scrupulously the generally accepted language of sales. In other words, while the difference between an 'opportunity' and a 'lead' might seem unimportant — such that you can tempted to simply scatter leads throughout the program in a haphazard manner — the lexicon used is actually tightly controlled. To make best use of the tool, it is therefore worth investing a little bit of time and effort in understanding typical sales processes.

Beyond including screens and entities for all the typical funnel stages which make it easy to manage and track the progress of the relationship with all the parties involved, many CRMs these days take a more visual approach to managing a sales process — providing dashboards with attractive diagrams that make it simplistic to understand the current state of a business's funnel.

Sales managers can therefore look at a depiction of a funnel and understand — at an eye's glance — exactly how much business might be coming next month or next quarter (and yes, in addition to being the CEO, Chief Doer, Head of

Accounting, Chief Cloud Architect, and Lead Marketer this is another title for you to hold!)

What a CRM Does

Okay, so enough about why you might *need* a CRM.

What exactly does it do?

Sadly, there isn't a singular answer to that very elementary question. And that's because there are so many CRMs on the market. I reckon that I've played around with 10 or so over the years, although there are only one or two whose functionalities I would say that I know deeply from years of use. But realistically there are probably at least a couple of hundred CRMs on the market, many of them targeting very specific niches.

Then there's the issue of differentiation that I touched on previously — which is something that you will see repeated in every crowded technology vertical. And CRM certainly qualifies as one of them. Every CRM naturally tries to put a spin on the traditional concept in order to differentiate itself from its competition — leveraging artificial intelligence (AI) to automate lead scoring is a popular one at the time of writing, for instance, but there are many others.

Nevertheless, and despite this sometimes artificial diversity, the following features, in addition to those which I have mentioned so far, could be regarded as particularly core:

- **Integrated inbox management.** Managing your email from an inbox — whether that's accessed from an internet webmail client or a desktop tool like Mozilla

Thunderbird — is fine. But only up to a finite point in the scaling journey. If your freelance business begins to scale, to the point where you need to enlist the services of a virtual assistant (VA) (or two or three of them), you'll likely want to begin sharing the process of nurturing leads with another human — or even a sales team. The big enterprise CRMs, like Salesforce, allow you to automatically route inbound queries through the CRM — configuring precise logic to ensure that the lead is passed onto the best account manager. In situations where there are hundreds of account managers, each with precisely defined sales territories, this is an essential feature rather than a nice-to-have. But it has advantages at smaller levels of scales too — such as the modest one which we are talking about throughout this text. By sending and receiving correspondence from contact pages rather than an inbox you'll be able to see a piece of correspondence — such as an individual email — as part of the broader context within which it fits: that of an ongoing relationship with the customer (getting the name, now?). In the effusive terms with which marketers often describe their product offerings these days this might sometimes be termed '360 degree viability'. Often what this means, deglossed of that somewhat delightful marketing spin, is simply that other elements of the tech stack — say, a ticketing system — are integrated with the CRM so that all the pieces of the digital jigsaw fit tidily together and one can look all around to see the various touchpoints where the lead has interfaced with your company. This means that the agent handling correspondence with the client, for instance, can see the contents and status of any tickets that the prospect or customer may have open with the support team — as well as a complete ticket history. A previous order history might be there too. As well as a recording of their last video call with the in-house customer success expert. If you ever feel like you've had to repeat the same information over and over again to successive customer service agents at a company, then you can understand why this is also highly advantageous from a customer experience (CX) standpoint — and why proper use of the CRM and logging by users is particularly important. To bring this down to a more personal level, imagine that you had a file you could call up on your desktop for your best friend. In this file you could see every piece of communication that the two of you had ever exchanged: the text messages, the emails, the messenger chats. You could leave annotations, for your own reference, at various intervals. You could set yourself reminders to reach out to your friend at a certain time. You could append documentation related to your friend into this personal dossier of sorts. You could even pass the file over to your personal assistant who could manage that relationship on your behalf. And, if you decided to pick up the phone and give your friend a call, you could do so in such a way that the call recording would be stored within the CRM. If you were to forget about this friend for a year and then try to pick up on the relationship, you could leaf back through this incredibly rich log, bring yourself quickly up to speed on where you left off, and then — directly from this system — jot your friend off a quick warm-up email. Imagine that you could repeat this process with *every* significant relationship in your life such that you never had to truly bother with things like email inboxes or messaging apps ever again. Everything would, rather, be there tidily encapsulated in the one place and you'd just have to get really good at interfacing with this one tool. You could even created automated workflows to cross-update records and describe relationships between the various types of stakeholder that you might routinely engage with. This, in essence, is much of the power of CRM.

- **Template management:** As I mentioned before a large part of one's time as a freelancer is going to be spent looking up companies that might need your services and sending them emails suggesting yourself as their next vendor of choice for X. Over time, as you build up a reputation and network, your need to be actively looking for business will hopefully lessen. But the early formative years of many a freelancer have been characterized by endless amounts of coffee, plenty of cold emailing, and an enormous side helping of grit.

- **Automation:** Despite chugging those liters of coffee, crunching through those spreadsheets, and spending those hours digging up the perfect point of contact at your target company, at the end of the day you're left with two hands and one brain to make the best of. A good way to do more with your limited supply of your most precious commodity (time) is to leverage the power of automation to your advantage. Most CRMs that I have either used or tested include this feature somewhere in their offering — although some parsimoniously reserve any kind of decent automation/ workflow functionality for only the top paying tier (we'll look at open source CRMs presently and this is one of many reasons why they sometimes make more sense: you don't have to scrimp and save, or deal with irrational artificial feature limits designed to facilitate upselling, in order to get the functionalities that you need to succeed). An automation engine will often be described as a workflow builder. Whatever it's marketed as its intention is usually to run automatic actions based on a predefined set of conditions. This can be either simple rule based logic. Or — in more sophisticated tools — the growing power of artificial intelligence (AI) can be tapped to allow synthesized human brainpower to autonomously execute basic decision-making. This could be, for instance, deciding whether a certain lead has a high or low likelihood of converting to becoming a paying customer. Automation rules can be used to do just about anything — including taking internal backoffice type actions. For instance, you could set up a rule such that all leads that you have identified as belonging to a certain industry are handed over to your VA — and your VA will receive an email notification when the lead is passed over. This kind of custom field and module building, to have the CRM organize your relationships along lines that mirror your organization's unique business flow (even if that's just you!), is really (again) where a lot of its value and power lies. CRMs are fundamentally elaborate relational databases — with a defined set of data held in tables and relationships between different entities and with fields that can be programmed to automatically update and otherwise interact with one another. Whether the taxonomy for those entities is reporters and media outlets (say, a CRM designed for the needs of PR practitioners) or political parties and candidates (a political CRM) is of almost inconsequential importance to understanding the concept of what the software is designed to do well. A whole ecosystem of specialized CRMs has developed — many of which are highly adept at addressing the use-cases and workflows that the niches they target commonly throw up. But the central premise underpinning the vast majority of them is that managing contacts is rendered much more efficient when done form a centralized system with the rough set of functionalities that I have described here.

- **Reporting:** Key Performance Indicators (KPIs) remain an important concept in the goals-oriented sales world. But you can leverage the power of goal-setting as a freelancer too! Most CRMs give you the ability to automatically, or manually, generate reports which give you insights into your sales activity. These might be cookie cutter reports which the CRM makes available as a library to all users or else individualized ones which you have built for your own needs — honing in on only those metrics, and trends, which matter to you. A CRM report could be as simple as a daily count of the volume of outbound email - which the CRM can measure as the number of emails which it passes out to through your outbound email (SMTP) server. You can set yourself a daily target and hold yourself to account if you fail to meet it. When you're your own boss, little tricks like this can make a huge difference in helping to keep yourself on target and motivated to succeed.

- **Logging:** If, again, you reach the stage where you can work with assistants and hired salespeople then this advantage will become apparent. As we have seen, a core feature of CRMs is the ability to log the information stored — and then share that with a team so that the burden of managing every relationship doesn't all fall on one person's shoulders. In more advanced setups, such as the one I described above with our best friend, CRMs can integrate with a VoIP tool — such that even telephone conversations held with customers can be logged in their appropriate entry so that they can be listened to by you (or another agent) and played back directly within the tool. The ease with which information can be shared with other people is another power of CRM (and, of course, user access permissions can generally be granularly managed for compliance and data protection purposes). The rest of the power is in the customization and the gathering of disparate information sources into one unified view.

Open Source: The Pros and Cons

Why Go Open Source?

We paused our discussion on setting up infrastructure aboard our hosting platform after looking at Softaculous — which, we said, makes it easy to install server scripts without having to worry about things like creating MySQL users and setting up configurations between the database and the files that comprise the actual program.

Softaculous's library includes a number of CRM scripts which can be installed on your hosting server in order to provide a similar set of functionalities to those which you might encounter in the SaaS marketplace. Vtiger, Sugar CRM, SuiteCRM and Yetiforce are just a few of the commonly installed options — although the projects are at various states of development (and in the open source world, deprecation always looms as a threat).

Although Softaculous makes it easy to install these scripts, there are plenty more than exist in its library — you'll just have to handle the installation process manually (a process we discussed in the previous chapter). Each installation also typically has a set of prerequisites and dependencies: packages you'll need to have installed on the server in order to ensure that the script provides the functionalities it is intended to. In a typical shared hosting environment, as I mentioned, you won't be able to request the installation of these packages if your host hasn't provided them in its default configuration — and yes, that applies even if you ask especially nicely. If you want to see what's out there then search for the software that you're looking for along with the keywords 'open source' or 'self hosted.' Some companies offer *both* SaaS and open source versions of a product. In these instances, the open source tool is often called the community edition (this is the nomenclature that Sugar CRM uses, for instance — at least at the time of writing).

Although the approach certainly has its limitations, for many, going open source and running their own cloud software has made a significant difference to the success of their freelance businesses and allowed them to access advanced tools for a fraction of the cost of SaaS programs — or, in some cases, even for nothing at all.

There are several advantages to using an open source CRM as well as several disadvantages.

Let's look at both in turn.

Advantages of Open Source / Self-Hosted Scripts

Cost

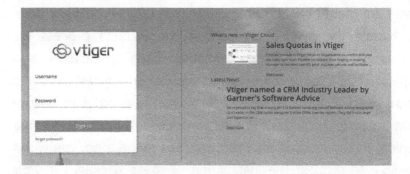

The big advantage to running open source software on your host is that it is typically free to do so — although this is not always the case.

When you are running software on your own server (even if it's technically that of your host, which you are renting) it is known as a "self-hosted" solution. This type of configuration is also commonly used to run programs on servers which are managed locally rather than through a third party on the cloud. Consider, for instance, intranet applications. This latter case is called an "on premises" installation, which is commonly simply referred to as "on-prem" (in case the etiology wasn't clear: the server hosting the application is physically located within the business premises).

Responsibility for Updates

Irrespective of whether you're self-hosting a CRM through your host or on-prem, you're going to be responsible for making sure that it's kept updated.

This isn't simply a matter of ensuring that you're always running the latest version with the newest features. Out of date scripts are a major security hazard and a common cause of successful web hacks: vulnerabilities are typically patched as they are discovered, and running a legacy version of a popular application might make you a sitting duck for cyberattacks who can quickly pick up on clues that the version of a script you are running is not the latest version and thus unsecure (remember the concept of caging and isolating file systems: hosting an application and your main site in the same directory makes this scenario even riskier because, if infected, damage can spread to other files within the directory).

This doesn't just go for relatively obscure server scripts such as Sugar CRM, however. Wordpress is a server script too — and because of its ubiquity it remains a highly popular target for SQL injection and other forms of hacking.

When dealing with the low hanging fruit of the cloud-hosted world — such as Wordpress — one needs to be especially diligent about adhering to security best practices. Keeping the Wordpress core and all themes and plugins updated is essential — and this can be configured automatically. Likewise, you should install a plugin that protects against brute force login attempts. And you should also add two factor authentication (2FA) to your login settings for improved security. This guidance isn't specific to the better-known cloud applications such as Wordpress, Joomla, and Drupal, however. You need to make sure that whatever software you are running on the cloud is kept continuously up to date just as you would ensure that your desktop was properly secured by authentication and all software on it was kept updated. The consequences of being derelict in these responsibilities are serious and potentially far-reaching. In the event that a script you are running *is* hacked, for instance, you could find yourself kicked off your host for, say, inadvertently operating an affiliate link website that the attacker injected so that he can piggy-back on your online real estate to make kickback dollars! The responsibility to ensure the security of your online empire rests squarely on your shoulders — not those of your host — and reading the fine print, in most cases, will make this abundantly clear (the same thing generally goes for taking backups, and we'll cover that later).

One final tip.

If you took my recommendation to install Cloudflare on your site, then you might also want to check out a tool that the company offers called Cloudflare Access.

Cloudflare Access allows you to protect certain parts of your website like *yourdomain.com/crm*. Anybody that tries to access this page will be presented with a login challenge: The easiest way to let yourself in but not anybody else is to configure for a one time password (OTP) to send to your email address, although you can also allow access for any user on a domain (this latter wildcard approach is an elegant and excellent means of sharing your portfolio with prospective customers who all work at the same company although the pricing might make this financially unfeasible). If somebody tries to put in anybody else's email address they will not be able to access to the application, like a CRM, that you are protecting.

The Cost Advantage of Open Source

Let's come back, for a moment, to the cost advantage of open source.

Self hosted software, like the Vtiger CRM, is often free but this is not necessarily the case or necessary for the definition.

Paid software can also be delivered via this means too. And it is possible that in these cases the total lifetime cost of ownership will still be substantially cheaper than paying for monthly or yearly access to your typical SaaS platform.

Whatever the payment model, the difficulty of keeping the script updated varies considerably in complexity between tools.

Due to its popularity, Wordpress can be updated virtually instantaneously and at the click of a button from within the backend — it's designed, after all, to be easy enough to use that those without sysadmin training, and who have never heard of an FTP account much less connected to a web server using one, can do whatever it takes to keep the program updated. Other update processes, however, are not quite so straightforward and beginner-friendly; some require following detailed documentation and uploading or replacing files manually. It's a good idea to investigate these matters *before* deciding on a technology that might end up becoming an integral part of your stack. Vendor lock-in and inertia remains a threat even if your solutions are simply free tools you picked up on the internet.

The final advantage to running software on your own server is that, in most cases, you have full control over the product — something which, as we saw, is clearly lacking in the SaaS model. In most cases you can literally see the code making the product run and adjust it as you see fit. If you would like to do that but avail of professional help to make the job easier, ecosystems of freelance experts and consultancies have built up around most major SaaS tools as well as open source platforms. And if there's something you'd really like your CRM to do but it doesn't work out of the box there's a good chance you'll be able to find a talented freelancer who can work on making an integration work for your or who can add a crucial missing functionality to turn it into a perfectly fitting tool for your business needs.

Yes, the update cycle mightn't be rapid (or even continuous) as it may be when using a SaaS platform. But on the flip side you'll have the ability to inspect what makes the software tick. And as mentioned, if you need it, paid help is usually just a few enquiries and a freelancer away. Just don't be surprised if these advanced services come at a premium.

Disadvantages of open source scripts

Let's look at the flip side of that question and see what disadvantages deploying your own software on the cloud might entail.

For one, as we have seen, you're responsible for managing the software yourself.

When you sign up to a typical software as a service (SaaS) platform like Salesforce (somewhat like when purchasing web hosting) you are paying for Salesforce to maintain a team of experts to keep the product constantly updated, patch vulnerabilities, and ensure the overall cybersecurity of the service in order to protect that data that you have stored in the application. If you are managing the software yourself, then you don't have that external talent pool working in your best interests and thus your data may be far more vulnerable. Instead, you're the cloud architect, CTO, and tech support wizard all rolled into one. Notice the trend here? Having to be a jack-of-all-trades — even within the various 'departments' of your business — is one of the toughest aspects of freelancing that I mentioned in the introduction.

The other major disadvantage is that, in many cases, SaaS products are simply far better than open source tools —

particularly those that are offered for free. For the past number of years, SaaS has been a major delivery model for business software — and there are no indications that that trend is going to change or even abate any time soon. Some speculate that, in time, *all* software will move to the cloud (others say the same thing about operating systems as we saw earlier) — although there are many applications whose resource heaviness precludes widespread adoption given today's typical internet connectivity (and that goes for even the business-grade ones which we explored in chapter one).

The Advantages of Going With The Flow

Whatever the future may hold, although you might be able to realize substantial cost savings by adopting an open source first approach, over time you might find that your business is in fact better served by adopting a more conventional tool with a wide user pool.

That latter point brings with it its own set of ancillary advantages: Where there are more users there tends to be a bigger community to tap into for peer-to-peer support and advice on how to make optimal use of the program (community support forums would be a salient example). The company that provides the software might even spin out a certification program — like Hubspot have done, for instance with their content marketing certifications — and passing those examinations and accrediting yourself with the qualification might open up professional doors for you that would otherwise have remained closed. Sometimes, thinking out of the box yields dividends. At other times, it doesn't pay to be a contrarian and swim contrary to the rising tide of cloud computing and software delivered through it as a service.

Choose whatever solution is best for your business at a particular moment in time. But keep one eye firmly on the future when doing so. Migrations can be a pain and inertia, as mentioned, is a very real factor to grapple with one you've been using a tool for a number of years and you — and in time those you work with — become very accustomed to things being as they are. Choose something that serves your needs well — and which is likely to do so for the foreseeable future too.

Cold Emailing Platforms

As we have seen, CRMs are sophisticated platforms that are designed to handle many facets of relationship management and ongoing engagement with customers. However, if you are in the trenches of trying to drum up business in the more immediate future (and at scale) then they are not always the ideal tool for the job.

Cold email marketing tools are a separate product category to CRMs. Tools like Klenty, Woodpecker, and many others like them are designed to do once thing well: Send out mail merges and automate drip email campaigns — and to do so, if required, at potentially massive levels of scale. These tools provide a number of additional features designed to maximize the effectiveness of cold email marketing — such as A/B or multivariate testing and altering the drip campaign based upon detected recipient actions such as email opens, clickthroughs, and replies (I'll leave my thoughts about the ethics of open rate tracking for another forum).

Unlike CRMs, they do not typically contain lead views for engaging with an interested contact one to one. That's what a CRM is for and the platforms expect that you will either handle that aspect of the lead nurturing process manually or through a CRM tool. Rather, their focus is simply on facilitating the ingress of lists of leads (typically, these are imported in comma separate value format) and then automatically sending out the emails (whether once-offs or as drip campaigns) designed to spark up a conversation. These tools know how to navigate cold email *really* well. Rather than send out emails all at once, for instance, they typically contain a sending interval function that can even sometimes be randomized. The idea is all to convince mail servers and mail transfer agents (MTAs) that your activity does not represent a major spamming effort (and, of course, it should not!) These are features that are typically lacking in CRMs which are not usually designed with mass mail merging in mind.

Although they can be used as self-standing tools, many of the email automation platforms *integrate* with CRMs so that you can use the two in tandem and synergistically. For instance, every new lead that you create in your CRM can be funneled into an email marketing cadence via an integration. If the lead expresses interest in your outreach, as we have seen, you can then move onto nurturing it via the CRM.

Cold email marketing, of course, needs to be done appropriately and in relatively sparing volume in order to be effective and not fall afoul of anti-spam systems.

Both data protection directives, like the Generation Data Protection Regulation (GDPR), and anti-spamming laws, such as the CAN-SPAM Act, also need to be kept in mind in order to stay compliant with the various third party technology providers (like dedicated SMTP services) that you may need to use as part of these efforts.

The main guiding principle at play is that if you cold email at all then you should do so judiciously: Ideally carefully screening your targets, only emailing the most relevant leads that meet your lead qualification criteria, and making it easy for leads to opt out of your database if they wish to do so (an opt out button is ideal but at a bare minimum you should inform recipients that they can communicate their volition to be removed from the database at any time — and that you will honor that request if only manually). You shouldn't retain the data that you collate in order to build cold email marketing campaigns beyond a reasonable minimum period of time (this is referred to as ensuring a reasonable retention period). Calling this 'data' may in fact be misleadingly reassuring and cause you to believe that the type of information which you might easily hold about subjects doesn't confer privacy rights on them if certain conditions are met (such as where the data is being stored, whether your data subjects are citizens of an EU member state or not, and where your business is based). A simple three column CSV file containing simply first name, last name, and an email address for instance might well afford those individuals whose contact details you hold rights under that legislation. 30 days is a good maximum retention period — and the information not required should be electronically deleted after it is no longer required.

Where does legitimate low volume cold emailing end and spam begin you might be wondering?

The line might seem a little blurry to some, but there are guidelines that can be offered if only in general terms. For instance, if personalizing every email isn't practicable, then you should at least focus on customizing the templates and focus on clearly demonstrating why it made sense for you to make the approach. Keep the contact list short and relevant. And, as I mentioned, make sure to present a clear opt out mechanism upon the first communication — if you are storing the contact information in a digitally mechanized database such as a CRM or cold email marketing tool. This is only a high-level sketch of the kind of nuances in the email copy and technical policies that are advisable in order to try to stay compliant with the various frameworks governing this facet of online marketing of course.

Woodpecker, and others, have put together useful resources addressing the topic in greater depth. I suggest reviewing them before engaging in any cold email marketing campaign — even if you simply opt to run it from a simple webmail client and without using specialized technology such as these cold email sending systems.

Email Marketing Systems

Going out touting for business all over the internet is well and good. But sometimes it's easier to let the customers come to you.

Inbound marketing is a whole field worth exploring for this reason: It includes doing things like content marketing and offering value-laden content to your target audience to position yourself as a trustworthy source of information. It can be used alongside outbound marketing — or you can focus on it instead as your main form of marketing activity.

The rough gameplan at work with inbound marketing is that, by delivering value to your prospects, you will kickstart a sort of symbiotic relationship with them. They'll scoop up your terrific insights about wedding photography (to provide an example of a credible freelance gig you might be selling). And when, in turn, they come looking for a wedding photographer, you're going to be top of mind — either for their own wedding or for their friends' one. That's a rough summary. And there's a lot more to it than that needless to say.

One of the key tactics that you'll probably want to look into for running an inbound marketing apparatus is offering an email newsletter — the same kind of thing that you've certainly received countless times after signing up for some product or service online. And for this you might want to avail of the services of some kind of email marketing program.

What Email Marketing Systems Do

Programs within this software category typically allow you to build, and segment, lists of contacts to whom you will be sending marketing communications.

Most of them will require that the contacts either opt themselves into the list, such as by signing up at an online collector, or ask that you certify that you have their express permission for sending email to them.

In other words, they do not support cold email contact and, if used for that purpose, you can be easily detected and flagged for a TOS violation (or summarily removed from the platform).

They often also contain some supplementary features — such as the ability to build, and display, landing pages.

In order to actually send the emails on your behalf you usually need to provide them with details to your outbound mail server (SMTP) — although others, like Mailchimp, work around that requirement through other technical means.

These can be used as part of lead generation campaigns — and you might want to also consider leveraging a lead magnet in order to maximize this strategy's effectiveness (a lead magnet is a resource, like a short e-book, that you offer your prospective customers in exchange for them providing their contact information to you. After they have agreed to the exchange, you maintain their details and can add them to your email marketing campaign).

Mailchimp is a free tool that should be good enough to get going with — although there are lots of other great options too. If you want something that you can host on your own server, then check out a tool called Sendy. Remember when I said that there were self-hostable tools that are commercial paid applications? Sendy is a great example of the kind of tool that I think you may wish to at least consider as a lesser known but potentially powerful alternative to a more famous SaaS counterpart. At the time of writing there's a one time licensing fee to pay. After that, the application is all yours to stick on a server and use it to tear up the internet with your enticing and informative email marketing newsletters.

Once you're set up on a tool such as Mailchimp, besides creating and managing a newsletter, you can create an automated onboarding email which you can automatically send to new clients as soon as they join your list. This is something that you should definitely consider setting up.

Mine thanks them for joining my client roster, provides a link to my payment information, which is on my website, and outlines the basic terms and conditions of the services that I provide, unless they are superseded by a contract.

As with so much of the technology we have been looking at, the idea is to provide a system that scales — and to save me having to send the exact same communications time and time again (a side benefit of this, and structuring most of your emails around a core template sent form a CRM, is that you can minimize the potential for human error.)

Dedicated SMTP Servers / Email Delivery Providers

I mentioned SMTP servers earlier.

And I did this because you're going to need to get the word out somehow that your freelancing business is ready to receive its first customers. Given that email has emerged as one of our predominant forms of communication (and cold phone-calling, by comparison, has diminished even further in popularity) it makes sense to have the technology on hand to .... send email with.

The Simple Mail Transfer Protocol (SMTP) is the standard protocol today for sending email. When we went on a whistlestop tour of the various components that a typical hosting package typically contained I explained that there is, generally, a full-fledged system for sending and receiving email at your domain just waiting for you to use. This system, however, is hosted on general purpose server infrastructure managed by your hosting company — as the fact that it is controlled through the cPanel your host provides would suggest. Additionally, the webmail clients that your host typically expects you to use with its built-in email system — such as Horde and Roundcube – well, let's just say that, by today's standards, they're not exactly works of UI art.

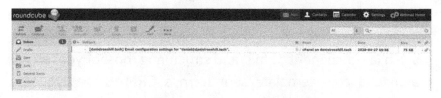

For this reason, relatively few customers chose to avail of this service and most edit their DNS records (specifically the MX entries which route email) in order to manage their email through some third party service. As I mentioned earlier, G Suite and Office 365 are two popular applications for this purpose — although there are smaller competitors such as Zoho (among others) vying for users' business too.

While using a third party service like this for email deliverability will almost certainly result in a more pleasant user experience than that which your host provided through the built-in tools, these services are certainly *not* designed with bulk email marketing use in mind. And again, while I don't suggest that you engage in cold email marketing activity in bulk, there *are* reasons why you might prefer to engage the services of a third party (or should that be fourth party) email delivery service.

The difference between sending your outbound marketing email through a G Suite SMTP server and, say, Sendgrid (a marketing-oriented email delivery service) may seem slight. But there are actually compelling reasons why opting for the latter approach is preferable in many instances. For one, Gmail (or G Suite) SMTP services are intended for personal individualized sending — and have rate limits to reflect that. Tools such as Sendgrid, and others in this product category, can scale into an entirely different stratosphere of volume.

Additionally, Sendgrid and other email delivery services are configured, out of the box, to support programmatic email delivery. As a result, most of them allow you to configure multiple API key credentials for the same sending address. Even at the small freelance level of scale this can be useful if you would like to delegate sending access to multiple virtual assistants (VAs). Each could be given an API credential, for instance, which could be connected, in turn, to a regular email client or a CRM. In the event that you no longer wish to grant a VA the ability to send email in your name all you would have to do would be to revoke that particular API key and they would lose the ability to send through any means.

Clearly, this way of managing access to your outbound email is far more granular and scalable than what you could achieve using a system like G Suite (or Gmail) which is clearly intended to simply allow one human to manage his or her email correspondence in a non-automated manner. However, you will still need to make sure that you are staying compliant with their terms of service (TOS). Most of these services will *not*, for instance, support cold email and make the usual requirement that they can only be used to send email to a list that has opted in to your communications.

Invoicing and Accounting Tools

After going through the grueling business of convincing somebody to hire you and doing your best work for them it's time to start turning out invoices in order to get paid.

Invoicing software and accounting platforms allow you to maintain invoices and then send them to your clients. The difference between the two is relatively self-explanatory. Invoicing platforms are generally just intended for maintaining and sending invoices while accounting systems are more full-fledged tools for maintaining accounts. Whether you're using one or the other, good ones usually also include an integration library to allow you to move data between them and third party services.

The Power of Integrations (And APIs)

Integrations, between technical services, allow you to use the services of two technologies in a complimentary, and sometimes synergistic, manner. For instance, an invoicing platform might have an integration with Paypal. Once you "connect" your Paypal account with your invoicing platform, you might be able to display a "Pay with Paypal" button at the bottom of your invoices.

Additionally, the invoicing platform might be able to automatically generate a receipt the moment that your client pays via Paypal. All of this can work to speed up the process of getting paid and saves you time by not having to write up receipts (if your country's bookkeeping standards mandate that, that is).

Both open source and SaaS invoicing and accounting platforms exist. And Quickbooks and Basecamp and are two popular options.

Project Management Software

As your freelance business gets busier, you might find that it gets harder to juggle the sometimes competing demands of multiple clients — which often seem to dovetail, inconveniently, around your biggest account's sudden urgent deadline.

Freelancers commonly use project management software, and to-do lists (task management programs) in order to make the job of keeping on top of everything that bit easier.

Again, both SaaS and open source models exist for this and approaches vary from Kanban style boards (Trello) to more full-fledged project management tools that, on higher tiers, allow you to engage in more sophisticated project tracking by mapping out task dependencies, showing critical paths from where you are now to project completion, and plotting everything tidily onto industry-standard diagrams such as the well-known Gantt charting system.

Of course, a calendar system — and a contact book— are also vital for staying on top of deadlines and setting appointments with clients (and keeping to them)

If you've signed up for G Suite, or Office 365, then these programs offer both of these functionalities. If you don't, then there are some other cloud scripts you can use which can host an DAViCal server (CalDAV and CardDAV are two common protocols for serving calendar appointments and contact information; WebDAV, as I mentioned, is a common protocol for serving files). OwnCloud, which is sort of an open-source, self-hosted cloud collaboration environment, includes these components too.

Document Management Systems (DMS Tools)

If you're freelancing line of business involves generating a lot of documentation for your clients (I'm in the writing 'game' so squarely in that category) then a solution which allows you to conveniently aggregate those documents into a login area just for your clients' use might be well-appreciated.

Of course, you can simply choose to send documents by email. But you can also build modules onto your CRM, share a Dropbox resources, or host a document management system. ProjectSend is one cloud software that fulfills this function but there are several alternatives if that doesn't meet your needs. A more elaborate approach is to modify a tool such as Drupal to create dedicated login areas, at unique URLs, for each of your clients. Of course, if you are intent on rolling out such a solution, you will need to consider whether the development time involved in setting it up is justified by the usability benefit that this might have for your clients. And if you're thinking about rolling out a system like this be warned: Pushback may be in store. Many simply prefer that you work with their systems (like Asana) and will balk at any attempt to do otherwise.

Web Analytics Scripts

To optimize your marketing, you'll want to pay close and constant attention to how people interact with your website. Website analytics is the preferred means of gleaning this information — and presents data that you can use to optimize the layout of your site, the text it contains, and any other features that you think might be helping, or impeding, its purpose (presumably: landing you business).

Google Analytics is a very popular option in this respect, although you'll need a Google (Gmail or G Suite) account in order to sign up for the service. If you don't want to do that there are other web analytics scripts (some which connect to analytics dashboards you can self-host) that provide similar functionalities. All you'll need to do to get it to work is add tracking code to your site and you will be able to see — in real time — where the visitors to your website are located, what they are viewing, and how long they are staying on each page. Heatmap tracking can take this even further.

The exact way to implement analytics depends on which platform you have built your site on. But generally the documentation provided by the analytics tool is comprehensive and — if your skills are more advanced — you can even use an Integrated Development Environment (IDE) to save you ever having to embed code snippets manually (even if your website is entirely comprised of static pages folder-wide find and replace tools make it simple to insert snippets automatically into large batches of files.)

The above is a non-exhaustive selection of the various services that you, as a freelancer, might deem necessary or helpful to optimize your business. In addition to the above, you might, whether now or down the road, consider looking at:

- **A tool for drafting legal agreements** such as contracts. There are also tools which allow you to capture legally enforceable electronic signatures online.

- **A platform for generating and sending proposals.** If a client is sufficiently interested in hearing about what you have to offer, they may request that you send a proposal through. Alternative, you might be participating in a tender/bidding process — such as sending in a response to a Request for Proposals (RFP) opportunity. In this latter case, submitting a proposal is a necessary formality to simply be considered for the project.

- **A human resource management (HRM) system.** Again, this one might be a little down the line from where you are currently, but HRMs typically feature the set of tools that you might require in order to mange your workers or subcontractors. Typical functionalities include tracking attendance, keeping track of benefits accrued, and monitoring used vacation and sick leave.

- **A tool for tracking your expenses.** Expensify is commonly recommended.

- **A time tracking software** for recording time spent on projects which are billable by the hour.

- **A VoIP solution and a videoconferencing tool** for holding international calls. These days, Zoom is the normative choice — and, if you're a frequent user, its premium tiers add important features.

- **A virtual phone number provider.** These allow you to order and generate international phone numbers which you can use to forward calls from other countries (at local rates for the other party) and protect the identity of your actual phone number by masking it behind another number (much as Cloudflare hides the identity of your real server IPs by passing them through its proxies!). Some solutions allow you to also send/receive SMS from the number and also place calls which inherit the virtual number's caller ID. You can also do things like build phone trees and create 'forward me' style systems to pipe the call onto a second extension if the first does not answer it. If you travel abroad a lot, this can be a great way to mange a business line — you can change the receiving extension to whatever number you are operating locally at the time.

- **A Pomodoro timer.** Handy for productivity!

- **A KPI dashboard** to visually keep on top of your progress.

- **A password manager** for (safely) keeping track of login credentials.

In Summary:

- Software as a Service (SaaS) products are offered by technology companies that host software on their own servers and then make it available to users for a fee. It's a business model that essentially entails renting access to a software that is provided and managed by a third party — in the cloud.

- You can sometimes reduce your SaaS overhead by deploying your own server installations yourself.

- The 'cloud' refers to resources that are available continuously on computers that a user does not actively manage. Clouds can be private, public, or hybrid. Neither ownership nor location are the distinguishing criteria — a private cloud, for instance, can be operated offsite in a third party data center but access to it can be restricted to its owner.

- There are a variety of common SaaS systems which you might, as a freelancer, want to sign up for and use.

- Integrations are ways in which different SaaS products, and other tools, can 'talk to one another' (programatically). By doing this, users can realize synergies and leverage the power of automation. Many other tools, like CRMs, use automation to help users do more in less time. Sometimes — in the CRM world — these features are known as workflow builders. The level of sophistication entailed varies from being able to configure simple rule-based logic to powerful AI-assisted tools that leverage complex algorithms.

- There are advantages and disadvantages to running your own software in the cloud. While one can realize cost savings one also foregoes the professional management and troubleshooting that is inherent in the SaaS model. From a cybersecurity standpoint, too, hosting data in a professionally managed cloud application is probably, in many cases, a safer bet than attempting to replicate the process yourself with a smaller team with less resources.

5. BACKUPS

Preparing for when it all goes pear-shaped

At this point, we've fleshed out more than enough information to get you up and running technically as a freelancer or self-employed independent worker — potentially, in fact, for many years to come.

Starting with finding a decent internet connection and computer, we've bought some turf to call our own in cyberspace; we then edited DNS records to get the website connected to the computer hosting it in the cloud, and provisioned a website on the internet. We've also hopefully set up — and connected — the additional cloud software that we might require to do the miscellaneous things we'll probably need to be doing on a daily basis. Things like updating invoices, keeping track of our client projects, and sending out marketing campaigns and building landing pages that will keep new clients coming in the door (or keep us finding them). We may even have rolled out an engaging newsletter and — who knows! — we might be well on the way to building for ourselves a reputation as a trustworthy and reliable provider in whatever it is that we do. In other words, we've started to leverage the power of inbound marketing to drive business to us.

Of course, there's a lot more to getting the whole picture right than all that — although we've certainly invested a decent amount of effort in the initiative so far.

For instance, we'd probably also want to set up various social media channels in order to, again, get our name out there and attempt to attract prospect clients to do business with us; set up a blog (if we didn't choose Wordpress as our main CMS - if we did we can just set one up there); and play around with a selection of additional services, like Hunter.io, to do things like dredge up email addresses for the people that we think might be interested in our services.

Of course, you'll also probably want to learn a little bit about SEO and search engine marketing and you may even want to dabble in running paid digital advertising campaigns or do a little bit of PR if you think that you are doing something interesting enough that it might win you earned media coverage.

Those are all important activities and very much a part of the picture. But there isn't much to be said, from a technical standpoint, about how to get all those components up and running. So for that reason I'm leaving that job to other authors and to your own process of trial and error.

The More You Stand To Loose, The More Important A Backup Regime Becomes

But before we go any further, let's look into how we might protect all the hard work that we've invested up to this point — so that almost no adverse scenario, however cataclysmic, is enough to render us down and out.

There are good reasons why we might wish to be especially prudent about our approach to backing data up. As a freelancer, our safety net might be far less robust than those which our friends in the corporate world enjoy (there's no IT department to call on for help, for instance, if we accidentally delete a treasure trove of files — we just better hope that we had the foresight to develop some system to help us recover from that eventuality before it was required!). So it's extra important that we take as many steps as possible to keep ourselves digital protected. And one quick specific recommendation in passing before we get into general good backup practices: if you're a freelance writer it's a prudent idea to always export PDFs, or take screenshots, of all your online work — and keep these in a backup folder somewhere.

Websites vanish without trace, URLs break — and sometimes your amazing writing goes with it (I've seen all those things happen). Thankfully there are many good screenshotting tools. Look for a 'rolling' one to make sure that you capture all the page and consider using developer tools, if you know some HTML, to get rid of things like unseemly banner advertising before taking the export.

The Unlikely Can — And Often Will — Occur

Setting up new technology that yields appreciable benefits for your business and your productivity is a great and satisfying feeling. However, the more you set up the more you stand to loose if — for instance — your hosting company vanishes off the face of the earth, your home office is catastrophically destroyed in a rainstorm, or a family member mistakes that home server you're running your website on for a rectangular piece of disposable plastic and throws it out with last night's dinner (remember when we said that hosting sites on an old laptop wasn't usually a good idea!?).

Disaster might also ensue if your home power supply gets fried by a lightning surge. Or you simply fudge a keystroke and press the delete button on the root level of your Google Drive folder and then — somehow — manage to empty it from the trash too. Somebody's keeping a backup, right? You will certainly hope so! But unless you're retaining the services of a freelance technology assistant then this is another task that's going to have to fall squarely on *your* shoulders. And don't forget, as before, that this *truly is* going to be one of your jobs. Reading the fine print of some of the technology that you've come to rely upon might be an eye-opening experience. Scrutinize all the Terms of Service (TOS) agreements you've signed with all the cloud providers we've mentioned here the next time you are really, really bored. In many cases, you'll find that keeping reliable backups is something that your cloud providers *will* be doing — and you certainly should hope that they *are* — but which there are, quite deliberately, no legal guarantees made in respect of.

Why Backing Up Cloud Data Matters

Even if you're not the type to be constantly envisioning what sort of calamity might befall you and your data, for other and more practical reasons, many people prefer to keep copies of their own cloud data. I strongly suggest doing so and have outlined, a little, my rationale. But I'll provide a few more examples just to really tease out the point:

- **Accidental deletion:** Remember that hapless freelancer who pressed the wrong key on his keyboard and then somehow managed to also obliterate the files from the trash — thereby deleting an entire Google Drive folder, with terabytes worth of data built up painstakingly over many years? Believe it or not I've seen this happen —

and no, I wasn't the responsible party! In another instance an overzealous systems administrator navigating on a server might run a *"sudo rm -rf *"* command from the root of the server rather than the directory he (or she) though himself to be operating in — thereby obliterating absolutely everything contained on it recursively (in this latter instance, I cannot deny that I am the source of the example). Unless you feel like being in perpetual danger of losing every scrap of work you've ever done for a client, every spreadsheet you've ever painstakingly pieced together to take a look at what competitors are doing, and everything else you might be storing on your cloud storage — then I suggest that you take a backup of any and all storage irrespective of whether it's hosted on a cloud, on your computer, or on a Network Attached Storage (NAS) device attached to your local network. Accidental deletion is something that *you* should be protecting against. Your cloud providers, in many instances, offer no protection against it. This is one of those things that it's better to discover *before* that information is of interest to you.

- **Provider lock:** Have you ever signed up for a SaaS program, become highly dependent on it for some critical part of your business, and then woken up to an email from them stating that they've just been acquired, are raising their prices five-fold, and the features you rely upon to operate — like a CRM workflow — are now moving up to a tier that is well beyond your budget? Although these events are comparably rare they do happen from time to time. Keeping a copy of all the data that you spread around the cloud is prudent for this reason alone: In the event that you need to suddenly up digital sticks, you'll always have a recent copy of your data to bring with you and migrate to another provider.

- **Data destruction by third party apps:** We've discussed, briefly, integrations. And thanks to the proliferation of Application Programming Interfaces (APIs), which allow different programs to interface with one another programatically, these are continuously increasing in number. (And codeless, everyday-user-intended tools like IFTTT and Zapier are well checking out if you need to string together a bunch of connectors without wishing to get knee-deep in trying to manually connect API integrations). Giving third party services access to a primary data source, like your Google Drive data, can be a good way to leverage the power of automation. Getting different services to "talk to one another," in this manner can also allow you to achieve more. However, before you allow any integration, it's important to scrutinize exactly what you might be permitting by authorizing the connection between two different data repositories on the cloud. The well adhered to best practice is for the connecting service to display this information prominently in a window when requesting your authorization for the connection to the other service — and it's worth taking your time to go over exactly what the application is requesting before you click the 'approve' button. The risks that you have to watch out for are: to your privacy (can this application read and access all your files? If so, is this a reputable company?). And to the integrity of your data itself. Third party applications with a read/write permission (as opposed to view-only) can wreak havoc on your files if not configured correctly or if anything goes wrong during execution. This is the type of data destruction that we will, again, need to protect against with cloud backups. As before, in the event that the worst case scenario happens it will be *your* responsibility to deal with the consequences of any unintended programmatic destruction of data, overwriting of new files with old ones, irreparable data corruption, or even the propagation of ransomware from an infected source to another source that it integrated with. Be prepared to restore; take copious backups!

- **Disaster:** It's a very remote chance, but there's always a possibility that any cloud provider which you entrust your data to will one day dramatically and without warning implode — vanishing off the face of the earth and taking its users' precious data with it. In a more credible scenario, your cloud provider might suffer a devastating cyberattack causing it to lose all its users' data right before its own backup process was due to run. In any event, hoping that any third party has been diligently taking backups of its users' data is not a prudent strategy to rely upon. Although incidents of the nature described are relatively few and far between they *have* occurred. And so it is prudent to hedge against them.

Over the years, I've developed my own backup strategy to attempt to mitigate the variety of small but cumulative risks posed by all these scenarios. It's a work in progress but, at a minimum, I make sure to periodically back up my local computer, my web hosting, and the various bits and pieces that I have scattered — like most freelancers — among various cloud services. This might strike some as over-cautious or unnecessary — but, again, experience has taught me that every piece of data that is critical to your business should be backed up. Ideally twice. And particularly any data that you entrust to a provider that you don't fully trust or have some misgivings about.

What tools do I recommend using? I have refrained from endorsing specific products because many are operating system specific and the features they offer are often a matter of personal preference. I recommend that you focus, instead, on ensuring that your various data repositories are backed up in the manner I'm about to describe (3-2-1 compliant backups). But to paint a broad picture. There are low level tools that are either CLIs or CLIs with basic GUIs and which back up data sources at a very basic level (rsync, rclone). As well as similar tools, like duplicity, which support created encrypted backups out of the box. Using these well requires being able to understand the documentation provided and being comfortable enough in a terminal environment to be able to add remotes (destinations) and build the right commands, or Bash scripts, needed to achieve the backups you want to run. Then there are more user-friendly tools such as CloudBerry. Some of these follow a freemium model and, on paid plans, provide the storage space that you require as well as the technology to run the backup itself. These use GUIs and, needless to say, are much more user-friendly than the previous tools.

Ultimately, finding a software that should meet that standard should prove to be a simple exercise in comparing competitors and costs.

Backups vs Disaster Recovery

Backing up, of course, is only done in order to prepare for the day in which your backups might be required — to recover from catastrophic data loss, for instance.

Whereas the subject of backups is concerned with ensuring that proper backups are taken, disaster recovery is concerned with actually ensuring business continuity by restoring from those backups.

Therefore, proper backup protocol calls for the testing of the backups that you take in order to make sure that — if required — they will prove viable images from which to restore to normal operation. Some tools, like Clonezilla, includes image testers as part of the backup process itself. This is a feature that you should look out for during your evaluation of the market.

The 3-2-1 Rule for Backups (And An Example)

That leads me on nicely to the 3-2-1 rule which is sort of the gold standard for many in the backup and disaster recovery world. According to this rule:

- **You should backup every primary data source that you have two times.** When you add the original to that you should have three extant copies of each data source at any one time.

- **Those two (backup) copies should be on different storage media.** For instance, you shouldn't keep a backup of your hard drive on the same hard drive. If the hard drive fails, the backup which it contains on itself will clearly fail with it — and you would be back-up-less. Instead, you might consider backing up your primary SSD onto an NAS — or at least onto another SSD within the computer. And to get granular, there are additional small differences between all these options that make backing up to an NAS, and an external plug-in disk, slightly different. If the onsite backup is to an additional drive within the computer, for instance, a surge to that desktop would still potentially fry it. The NAS, by contrast, might survive a power surge to the desktop — especially if it is located in a different room on a different power circuit. But an external hard drive that is not connected to *any* electrical device — but rather sits, between use, in a filing cabinet — would survive any kind of adverse power event such as a surge. If you're regularly taking onsite backups then a drive enclosure — which lets you mount a full-fledged internal drive as easily as a USB device — is an additional peripheral that is worth purchasing.

- **Additionally, one of those copies should be stored offsite.** (This means somewhere that isn't colocated physically with your first backup copy.)

Let's break that down with an example.

Let's say you use a Windows laptop as your day to day computer. You should use a program and keep one backup copy of the data on that computer that you cannot afford to loose — say your files and folders containing the work you do for your clients.

You might choose to use a program that backs up just your user area or else one that captures everything on the computer (practically speaking, you almost never want to back up *everything* on a computer).

For argument's sake, let's say that your program generates a backup that you store on an external hard drive. But what would happen if your home was robbed, or flooded, and everything — including your laptop and your hard drive — were destroyed or stolen? It's scenarios like these — as unlikely as they may seem — that keep backup enthusiasts like me tossing and turning at night (when not worrying about unpaid invoices, that is).

The solution for the problem that I outlined is to keep another backup copy of your laptop offsite. Technically anywhere that isn't the same physical location (roughly) as your other backup copies will do the trick — but technically the further they are geographically dispersed the better.

For instance, you could make *two* copies of your Windows computer onto *two* different hard drives and then keep one in a chest of drawers in your office. That way, if your home is, again, flooded or robbed you would be able to buy a new laptop and then use the copy of your data which you keep at work in order to restore your critical data.

These days, however, commercial cloud storage has become extremely affordable — so rather than keeping hard drives in office cabinets most people store offsite backups in places like AWS S3 buckets instead (or in Backblaze B2).

These are known as cloud object storage providers and the form of storage that they offer isn't quite the same as the more familiar consumer-oriented platforms. Unlike, say, Google Drive, they're intended for larger scale storage of data and storing backups in these storage vaults is a common use-case. In some instances (like AWS Glacier) they offer lower data storage costs in return for making the data slightly less available and easy to access. Think about term deposit accounts versus current accounts in a bank: It's a very similar principle.

If you're backing something up offsite with a provider like AWS, then AWS actually already adds a lot of additional redundancy for you by storing copies of your data in various locations across its network— so you actually have a very impressive amount of redundancy working in your favor in addition to now having a backup copy of your data offsite.

If you use a commercial paid backup program then the program will probably bundle cloud storage with the software and you won't have to worry about *where* to put it on the cloud.

If you prefer a more DIY approach then you can sign up for cloud object storage and then use whatever utility looks best to you in order to move it to the cloud. If you're packing up cloud sources, then it's usually quicker to move things 'over the wire' — from public cloud to public cloud — otherwise your typical home internet upload speed becomes a frustrating bottleneck in your backup process. For object cloud storage, I highly recommend Backblaze which offers both backup plans as well as an affordably priced cloud object storage platform called B2. But AWS S3 is a good option too (among others).

Differential, Incremental and Full Backups

Cloud to cloud backups can run at lightning-fast pace across the wire, but what about backing up local machines and local servers? You might be wondering how people manage to get backups of these up to the cloud and whether server rooms and back up tapes are still a 'thing' — perhaps one you may wish to consider down the line.

Fortunately, taking regular backups also needn't mean moving gigabytes of data over slow internet connections.

Over the years, backup approaches have improved. And nowadays it's more common to backup only the files and folders that have changed since you last ran that backup. This is called running an incremental backup approach. And if you see this marketed in a backup software then what it means is that each time the program is running the backup copy is only being updated with the files that have been added, deleted and moved since the last run. By putting together a succession of these incremental slices together, it's possible to quickly restore data back to a historical point in time. The only negative to be aware of is that this (often) means that the various backup points have to be good. Differential backup is an approach somewhere between incremental backups and full backups (backing up the whole file system each time the program runs). When a backup program uses a differential approach each time the program runs it is creating a backup slice with all the chances to the filesystem since the last *full* backup was run. Naturally these are heavier 'slices' than the incrementals. But on the positive side only two chunks of data — the full backup and the differential — are needed for restore. A full backup means essentially what is says on the tin — backing up the whole file system every single time the backup job runs. Finally there are disk clones (sometimes known as disk images or bare metal backups). Unlike full backups these are often created from a live USB disk with the system cold. System images literally create an exact clone of a drive.

Regarding running local servers to store backups and data: it's still done, although probably something you won't want to do from the outset unless you're creating a lot more data than can be comfortably stored on your computer. In the business environment this kind of data storage is called 'on premises' — as we saw in the SaaS chapter. At the consumer level, something called a Network Attached Storage (NAS) is a popular option. Unlike, say, a generic server this is typically a prebuilt computer which you just need to add storage into. Unlike a server, it also usually comes with an operating system that makes it incredibly easy to install programs and software (such as email and mail servers). Finally, once you have your drives installed into an NAS the computer will typically set them up, through software, in something called a RAID configuration. RAID stands for Redundant Array of Independent Disks (RAID). It pools those physical hard drives into one logical unit (storage pool that looks like one unit). Unless you're using RAID 0, RAID offers redundancy and protection against disk failure. This means that in exchange for never being able to use quite the full amount of capacity that you installed in the NAS, the storage pool will be able to rebuilt itself in the event that one or multiple drives fail.

One final thing to worry about, no matter how you have your local data stored, is data degradation. Physically, over time, the quality of stored data can degrade. A thorough disaster recovery plan should factor this in and ensure that backups are regularly probed for restorability. And if you're not using an NAS, then the disks themselves should be regular tested for health. At the first sign of potential trouble, like bad sectors, it's time to immediately swap them out for new storage.

That's almost certainly more than you'll need to know for quite some time about backup and local storage — sometimes being a technical jack of all trades means just knowing the basics about a lot. The information above should be enough for you to know what you're trying to achieve by using the tools I've mentioned — and more importantly, to keep your data safe and well backed up

Backing up SaaS

Besides backing up your laptop, desktop, NAS, and local server (if you have one), I strongly recommend backing up whatever data that you have on the cloud — irrespective of whether it's a few to-do lists or a cPanel backup of your entire website. I've tried, but failed, to find a unified program that will do the heavy lifting of manually ingressing data from all the various cloud-hosted tools that I use. If you run a Google search for 'cloud to cloud backup' you'll find a few that come close to doing this — but you might have a hard time finding a provider that supports each and every service that you use and which also happens to support the exact type of storage media that you want to use as your destination/target (where you want the backups to be stored online).

Instead, like I did, you might need to develop your own proprietary backup approach if you are sufficiently worried — employing a mish mash of different tools to ensure that, no matter what happens to your primary data source(s), you will have some reliable means of springing back into action and preferably even a choice of backup sources from which to restore (and to be extra thorough, you should ideally test the restorability of all backups that you generate).

Finally, if you're backing up your cloud data don't forget about your cloud storage repositories: By which I mean things like Google Drive, Dropbox, Box.net, and pCloud. It's a little bit easier to find dedicated tools whose express function it is to move data between different cloud sources as a means of creating redundancy for one cloud onto another.

Just don't forget to download a copy to store locally in order to ensure that this data pool is 3-2-1 compliant too.

Destinations: Where To Store Your Backups

After successfully identifying your backup *sources* (the data you need to protect) you may be left wondering where all that data is going to *go*. In other words, your backup *destinations*. There are a few common options.

As we've seen, for offsite backups the best option is typically to back up to cloud storage. And, as we mentioned, we'll either want to use the storage that a backup program (such as CloudBerry) is best designed to work with (in which case we mightn't need to configure anything) or else we'll be purchasing space from an object cloud storage provider to host our backups.

If the amount of data that we're protecting is very small (say, a local user directory with mostly Word documents and presentations) then we may even be able to get away with backing it up to a more familiar form of cloud storage such as Google Drive or Dropbox. However, in general (and to avoid confusion) it's recommended to keep your cloud backups and cloud data separate (not doing this makes it a lot easier to accidentally back up other backups, thereby creating unnecessarily heavy files).   If you really like the user-friendliness of simple cloud storage platforms, consider setting up one account just for storing backups. Just check the TOS to make sure that using the space for this purpose is okay with the provider.

Where should you keep files that you back up locally — like your computer or its key files?

One option is to add a dedicated backup drive to the computer itself. You can either periodically keep your main drive and backup drive in sync. Alternatively you can do something a little bit more sophisticated and create a RAID 1 (Random Array of Independent Disks) synchronization between your main disk and another one that mirrors it. There are a variety of RAID types and this format is used widely in backups to protect against the constant threat of disk failure. RAID setups can be configured both using software (which results in a performance overhead) and by hardware controllers.

A simpler option is to simply buy an external drive — or else a regular drive and an enclosure — and periodically do something like take images using Clonezilla, which can be run from a live USB. Other users prefer to build a script and run a nightly job, using rsync and cron, to periodically run an incremental backup between the production and backup drives.

Finally, one can set up either a local server on the network or buy and provision a Network Attached Storage (NAS) device. NAS devices are designed out of the box with constantly available file storage in mind — and also usually allow the user to use proprietary software developed by the manufacturer. Typically, they feature bays in which users can slide in storage devices (like HDDs, SSDs, or NVMe SSDs) — and the device automatically uses a RAID configuration to provided redundancy. However, others prefer setting up their home servers simply because it allows them full control over what combination of software to deploy.

Whatever option you choose, it's advisable — as mentioned — to periodically pull down backups from the cloud, even if *those* files are themselves backups. Giving yourself plenty of storage is a good idea too. These days, storage is cheap (particularly if you're fine using hard drives). A small bit of investment in a great backup infrastructure can save a lot of time and money by averting technical calamities caused by unexpected and often devastating data loss. Finally — and as a security measure — you may want to encrypt your local backups, even if they are not encrypted on the cloud. Doing so prevents the possibility that, if somebody were to break into your home and rob your NAS or file server, they would be able to read and steal your personal data.

In summary:

- There are a variety of reasons why it makes sense to back up all your mission critical data. Accidental deletion, provider lock-in, and data destruction or corruption by third party integrations are just three of them.

- This applies to both local data (your computer) and data on the cloud.

- A good approach for effective backups is the 3-2-1 rule: you should keep two extant backup copies of all data. The two backup copies should be on different storage media. And one of them should be stored offsite.

- Taking good backups is generally your responsibility — and not that of those you are buying cloud services from.

6. SECURITY

Because it's important to stay safe

Finally, let's take a quick look at security — because increasingly, freelancers are also worried about making sure that they keep safe online, even if the projects they are working on are not likely to be flashing targets for those intent on pirating other people's work.

You've probably been hearing a lot about cybersecurity and the importance of keeping safe online. And we touched on a couple of these concepts earlier. But let me repeat them here in order to tie everything we have covered so far together.

The Importance of Two Factor Authentication

Firstly, login security.

If you're not already doing so, then you should definitely be using two factor authentication (2FA) on every single account that offers it — even if you might spend an extra three minutes a day copying and pasting authentication codes into browser windows as a result. You might have been seen a system prompt but decided not to set it up. Maybe you weren't sure what it was. So let me briefly explain.

The traditional paradigm for securing access to a web service, or just about anything on a computer (and you've probably been using this for a long time) is by providing a username and password. However, there's a vulnerability inherent in this approach which is worth thinking about. Hackers are sometimes able to simply attempt to take a vast amount of guesses at both credentials by programatically attempting different alphanumeric combinations until the correct one is found (this methodology is called brute force attacking; and naturally hackers use programs to shuffle through the various guesses). To make it much harder for hackers to illicitly gain access to services, most online services have started offering 2FA to their users — and some even make it a requirement.

The second credential which 2FA (sometimes called multifactor authentication / MFA) is named after might be generated by an authentication app (such as Authy or Google Authenticator). It might be a time-limited One Time Password (OTP) that is sent by email or text message (or sometimes even over a messaging service such as WhatsApp). Or it might even be a biometric identifier — such as a fingerprint scan or one delivered by a facial recognition technology. However it is delivered, the second layer of security is designed to make it a lot trickier for a malicious actor to take over your account.

In addition to figuring our your username and password, for instance, a hacker might have to figure out a way to copy your SIM card — or else siphon off packets directed for you in order to try see what they contain and abuse that knowledge to hack into your account (this is called packet sniffing; the limitation is that it generally needs to be done in close physical proximity to the target such as when the packet sniffer and his intended victim are both computing on the same local network).

These attack vectors require sophisticated knowledge and equipment — and that's only the start of the complications that this approach would entail for somebody intent on breaking in to a system that you operate. Therefore, most low-level hackers will not be capable of pulling off the hack — or indeed motivated enough to even begin trying.

Other Security Best Practices

Besides using 2FA, there are a lot of basic best practices that you should adhere to as a freelancer. For one, as mentioned, it's important to keep all your applications on the internet well updated. This step alone greatly reduces your changes of maintaining codebases with unpatched vulnerabilities that could serve as *"please attack me"* signs for those intent on doing so.

Running security and antivirus scanners on everything server-side is recommended too: both on your local machine (your laptop or desktop) and in the cloud. There are scanners and security products that are designed to be run on servers just as there is equivalent protection for desktop devices — even though the latter market is much more familiar to consumers. Somebody successfully hacking your laptop might lead to identity theft or make away with some files (if you're using a password manager locally, make sure to enable the master password for this reason!). Somebody that manages to deface your website with embarrassing messages — or who manages to take it down just when a prospective client is trying to access it — might in fact cause you more immediate adverse consequences as well as damage to your professional image and brand reputation. Therefore, in order to develop an effective security posture, both threats — to the local and cloud 'surfaces' — need to be constantly mitigated against.

And these threats, unfortunately, are not going away any time soon. To the contrary attack payloads, over time, only become more sophisticated and the threat landscape only widens to include both legacy threats and more sophisticated exploits.

Phishing scams, Man in the Middle (MITM) spoofing tricks, and botnet-mediated attacks including DDoS attacks all continue to be significant threats to many web users and corporations. And it is usually advisable to run a third-party application to expand upon whatever native capabilities your operating system might provide in this department.

Securing Connectivity and Anonymity: VPNs and TOR

But what about securing connectivity to the internet itself, you might be wondering?

Having a VPN is not essential although there are cases in which it is advisable (such as when you are browsing the internet from any untrusted network — remember that sniffing, man in the middle attacks, and packet sniffing are all often easier when you're using a network manged by somebody else, such as one which might be found in a public WiFi hotspot).

Some freelancers, but particularly journalists, are interested in using TOR (The Onion Router; a network designed to protect the identities of users and those operating servers) — particularly if they are engaged in producing journalism and speaking to sources based in undemocratic and repressive regimes.

Used in parallel with a VPN (which can obscure the user IP connecting to the TOR entry node) TOR can certainly provide heightened privacy and anonymity. But it should never be thought of as a perfect or foolproof system. Besides the omniscient threat that exit nodes could be subvertly monitored by governments, the traffic needs to emerge onto the regular internet at some point in its onward journey to the internet — although properly secured its contents should still be reasonably secure.

The Power of Encryption

Speaking of encryption — that's something you'll be hearing a lot about these days if you're interested in making it harder for the cybercrooks to rain on the party of your freelancing success.

Encryption is a pandora's box — and just about anything can be protected with basic encryption for those sufficiently motivated to use the tools required to make it happen: Entire computer drives, individual files, emails, and anything that you send over the cloud can all be encrypted and their contents obfuscated from plain text inspection.

Pretty Good Privacy (PGP) is a tool worth exploring if you'd like to leverage end to end encryption (E2EE) to secure email communication with a trusted sender from your usual email address. If you're fine with using a different, dedicated email address for this purpose then check out Proton Mail — a secure email client maintained, quite appropriately, by a Swiss company and which is accessed over a webmail interface that compares favorably to Gmail.

There are different standards of encryption and different methodologies for encrypting (end-to-end encryption, client-side encryption, and server-side encryption). If you're ever sufficiently concerned about the integrity of your data, you can do digging then to find out what those differences mean then. But no matter what guarantees a third party about what logs they keep (or don't keep) or claims they make about being a zero knowledge provider that doesn't make your keys accessible to their own employees — whether you feel confident enough to believe these claims and use a certain service ultimately boils down to a simple question of trust.

The main thing that most casual users need to know about cybersecurity is that when the a URL is prefixed by https:// the connection is reasonably secure (at least when on a trusted network). It is not a good idea to do much over a http:// connection these days — communications can be easily read as the packets travel across the internet (including by your ISP), passwords and usernames can be seen in plain text, and financial information can be seen by the naked prying eye too. Certainly don't buy anything online, or provide financial information through any means, if the connection doesn't display the padlock symbol — or the equivalent in another browser's UI.

Finally, if you don't really trust anybody else's computer and want to really stretch your security-consciousness (can you tell I'm relatively far along that spectrum?) you might want to consider burning a live USB containing a secure operating system that, by default, forces traffic out through TOR or some other network that provides decent anonymity.

Storage, when using a live USB is typically not persistent — so whatever changes you make on the file system will be lost by the time you plug the USB into another device.

Check out QubesOS for this purpose — or another option.

In Summary:

- Second factor authentication (2FA) adds an extra layer of security to logins by requiring the presentation of an additional credential in order for users to authenticate themselves with a provider. This can be generated by a software authentication device, by a hardware tool, or by a one time password (OTP) delivered by email, SMS, or over some other medium.

- Phishing scams and other online threats remain relatively commonplace. Equipping oneself with basic protective measures, like an antivirus and internet security tool, is prudent.

- This applies in the cloud too: there are security tools and virus and malware scanners intended just for running on servers.

- Securing the resources you run on a server, such as by keeping scripts well updated, is generally the user's responsibility. The consequences for being derelict about this duty include being removed from a hosting company's infrastructure.

7. TECHNOLOGY TRENDS

Because we all need to bluff sometimes

Hopefully the information contained so far will be enough to both orient you towards the various technologies you might be coming into contact with as a freelancer and keep your from feeling like a total Luddite if you have children, or grand-children, that are constantly raving about the latest tech craze. Particularly if you wake up the next morning to find that your main clients wants you to write a 2,000 word in-depth article on the difference between artificial learning and ML.

However, in truth, even children and grandchildren these days can get a bit bewildered by the various technologies that are constantly coming to market and stretching the bounds of what computers, and humanities, can achieve when working in tandem.

Because many freelancers are freelance writers — and technology remains a perennially attractive niche to write about — here's a quick primer, to conclude this guide, on some buzzwords and new trends that you have almost certainly already come across.

Artificial Intelligence (AI)

Increasingly, algorithms are being developed which aim to mimic, to some extent, human intelligence. AI is being applied to different industries to take away the mind-numbing grunt work that characterizes, at least in part, some jobs (I never said that freelancing wasn't included!). Machine learning (ML) is a subset of AI and allows machines to learn how to make decisions from a set of feeding data — without having to be explicitly programmed or supervised, in order to do so, by humans.

Augmented reality (AR)

Augmented reality (AR) enhances the environment that a human is in. For instance, a support technology that leverages AI might offer, as a feature, the ability to automatically annotate ports on photographs, or a video stream, that a technician sends up to the cloud or directly to a colleague. Virtual reality (VR), by contrast, aims to put the user into a virtual environment — one which is not real.

Blockchain

You've almost undoubtedly heard about cryptocurrencies such as Bitcoin. While that concept is revolutionary in its own right, the most paradigm-shifting aspect of the whole picture is actually the notion of blockchain — which is the technology framework that underlies the idea of currencies that are not created and administered by a centralized entity such as a bank or backed by that issuer's guarantee. In blockchain, databases (or rather, the ledger) is managed distributively by an enormous amount of 'nodes'. In a blockchain no block can be altered retroactively without the alteration of all subsequent blocks (hence the name). The potential applications for this, across industries, are great breathtaking.

The Internet of Things (IoT)

Traditionally, computing has involved human-manged objects, like a desktop, interfacing with other human-managed objects, like a server. The network that we know as "the internet" ensures connectivity — as we have seen — between all these components. The IoT aims to connect a vast amount of "things" to the internet and bring them online. Unlike the internet-of-non-things, these "things" are not computers designed for direct human interface like desktops. These could be, for instance, chlorine sensors in a smart water management network or smart fridges that have the ability to report stock levels of a certain food product to a cloud-hosted network — which, in turn, relays that information to the end-user. The first example was drawn from the industrial internet of things (IIoT) and the latter from the consumer IoT. Tangentially, the development and continued spread of the IoT has also necessitated the development of special radio networks equipped to operated at low power so that the devices that need to receive and transmit to them can stay active remotely for a reasonable period of time (replacing the batteries in thousands of remote sensors might clearly be a difficult endeavor that operators would be keen to avoid). The first example of the IoT I gave (the water network) is significant particularly because it represents a major target for cyberwarfare between nations. But because somebody that hacks into a home network with smart devices could also do very tangible mischievous things like turn off the user's fridge (or, much more grievously, unlock a smart lock ahead of a burglary attempt) the development of the IoT has also opened a new frontier in cybersecurity in both the consumer and industrial-oriented fronts.

Serverless

We touched upon cloud computing and various hosting configurations earlier in this text. Serverless is a concept in cloud computing in which backend resources, like servers, are provided on a dynamic basis — so that users can simply be charged for how much computing time they use. In other words — the servers that the provider provisions are themselves (physically) not fixed but rather made available on an ad-hoc basis to those that need them. This, in turn, allows companies to scale up and down their cloud workloads in a much more flexible manner. Kubernetes is a different technology, but also a hot topic in cloud computing right now.

www.ingramcontent.com/pod-product-compliance
Lightning Source LLC
LaVergne TN
LVHW041205050326
832903LV00020B/462